Southern Living
FAMILY FAVORITES
Style

163 HOUSE PLANS OF ELEGANT HOMES

Published by Hanley Wood
One Thomas Circle, NW, Suite 600
Washington, DC 20005

General Manager, Plans Services, David Rook
Associate Publisher, Development, Jennifer Pearce
Manager, Customer Service, Michael Morgan
Director, Marketing, Mark Wilkin

Editor, Simon Hyoun
Assistant Editor, Kimberly R. Johnson
Publications Manager, Brian Haefs
Production Manager, Theresa Emerson
Senior Plan Merchandiser, Nicole Phipps
Plan Merchandiser, Hillary Huff
Graphic Artist, Joong Min
Director, Audience Development, Erik Schulze

Hanley Wood Corporate
Chief Executive Officer, Frank Anton
Chief Financial Officer, Matthew Flynn
Chief Administrative Officer, Frederick Moses
Chief Information Officer, Jeffrey Craig
Executive Vice President/Corporate Sales, Ken Beach
Vice President/Finance, Brad Lough
Interim Vice President/Human Resources, Bill McGrath

Most Hanley Wood titles are available at quantity discounts with
bulk purchases for educational, business, or sales promotional use. For information,
please contact Jennifer Pearce at jpearce@hanleywood.com.

VC Graphics, Inc.
Creative Director, Veronica Vannoy
Graphic Designer, Jennifer Gerstein
Graphic Designer, Denise Reiffenstein
Graphic Designer, Jeanne-Erin Worster

Photo Credits
Front Cover and pp.5, (top) 49-53: ©Coastal Living Magazine/John O'Hagan;
Back Cover (top) and pp.3 (left), 4 (above and right), 5 (bottom), 6-10, 120-123: ©The Progressive Farmer/John O'Hagan;
Back Cover (bottom) and pp.3 (right), 4 (bottom), 87-91: ©Southern Living, Inc.; p.119: ©The Progressive Farmer/Rob Lagerstrom

Design
Cover and Book Design, Deana Callison for Southern Living

Distribution Center
PBD
Hanley Wood Consumer Group
3280 Summit Ridge Parkway
Duluth, Georgia 30096

10 9 8 7 6 5 4 3 2 1

Printed in the United States of America

Library of Congress Control Number: 2007930103

ISBN-10: 1-931131-75-9
ISBN-13: 978-1-931131-75-9

FAMILY FAVORITES

Sand Mountain, page 6

Poplar Grove, page 87

4 INTRODUCTION
Discover what distinguishes a Southern Living house plan from other predrawn home designs.

6 LESS THAN 2,600 SQ. FT.
In a variety of styles, these homes are ideal for smaller families or as vacation retreats.

49 2,600–3,000 SQ. FT.
Find dedicated spaces as well as flexibility in these just-right family designs.

87 3,001–3,500 SQ. FT.
High-end amenities and formal entertaining spaces will delight homeowners and guests.

119 OVER 3,500 SQ. FT.
Impeccable style, luxury finishes, and deep comfort arrive without compromise.

Southern Living
Style

163 HOUSE PLANS OF ELEGANT HOMES

CLASSICAL, COMFORTABLE, CHIC

For 20 years,

Southern Living magazine has been collecting exclusive home plans from the South's top architects and designers. From formal and elegant traditional homes, to casual and stylish cottages, the *Southern Living* plan collection has long been a favorite feature of the magazine for readers and admirers of southern architecture.

Above and Right: Sand Mountain is a smaller Colonial design with space-efficient features. See more of this plan on page 6.

Below: Poplar Grove will appeal to larger families looking for outdoor-living opportunities. Turn to page 87 for more photos.

This hand-chosen collection of 160 plans represents the very best family-sized designs from the entire *Southern Living* portfolio of over 800 plans, presented in book form for the first time ever. We feel that each home offers an attractive balance of historically influenced exteriors—Neoclassical, Colonial, Craftsman, European—and modern approaches to interior layout. Along with beautifully presented formal rooms, every plan recognizes the need for hard-working utility spaces, such as mudrooms, offices, pantries, and flexible-use areas. Covered porches, keeping rooms, and other seasonal spaces present easy opportunities for extended family gatherings and entertaining. On some plans, exclusive access to a porch creates a private retreat for homeowners.

The four sections of this book have been ordered by total square footage, each section opening with a featured design that exemplifies the advantages of a home of that size. For example, section one begins with Sand Mountain (page 6). Notice how the rear porch extends the central living area and master suite. The detached garage helps preserve the period look of the design from all elevations, as well as allows the home to sit on a smaller lot. At the other end of the spectrum is Stones River (page 119), a large contemporary farmhouse that still finds room for comfortably scaled personal zones.

The charms of a Southern Living house plan are like those of the South itself. Timeless grace, beauty, and a warm welcome await you.

Top: Sea Island House offers equal parts getaway charm and curbside poise. Read more about this home on page 49.

Above: A hanging bed feels right at home in Stones River, a contemporary farmhouse made for wide open spaces. This plan starts on page 119.

SAND MOUNTAIN

Southern Country Charmer

The ideal smaller home
for any neighborhood

Simplicity

and sophistication combine in Sand Mountain, a sprawling one-story plan with many charms. This plan honors the richness of traditional design elements with its covered, columned porches, multiple fireplaces, and distinctive exterior, and also showcases contemporary design features such as an opulent master suite, spacious home office, and easy outdoor access. A covered walkway connects the two-car garage with the home's rear entry.

Although the formal dining room, to the left of the foyer, is elegantly arranged and well-suited to entertaining, it's the family room that is the heart of the home. A towering stone fireplace serves as its focal point; other stunning elements include built-in bookshelves and cabinets, two doors that open to a covered rear porch, and a view of the loft area. Also noteworthy is the kitchen, with its perfect blend of form and function. Plenty of counter and cabinet space, an expansive range top, and conveniently located appliances provide multiple cooking stations, and a built-in wine refrigerator offers added convenience.

Set to the rear of the left wing, away from the main living areas, are an office, full laundry room, and very able mudroom. Architect John Tee considers this trio of rooms—the home office in particular—the plan's most noteworthy aspect. The office, Tee says, is "dedicated to a person who

Above: Overlooking the rear property, the nook is bound to be a favorite spot for family meals.

Below Left: The small covered porch at the back of the home can become a treasured living area. A shed dormer adds interest to the rear elevation.

Opposite: A stone fireplace and vaulted ceiling emphasize the attractive height of the family room.

works at home full-time," such as on a working farm, where the room would serve as the business office. Employees can easily enter and leave through the private entrance without having to pass through the residence; alternately, they can use the side entry, and stop in the mudroom before visiting the office. The mudroom, bringing modern convenience to the side entry, features a spacious reach-in closet, generous counter space, built-in cabinets, and a full sink, as well as proximity to a shower. And the laundry room, hard working as well as attractive, provides shelves, counters, and views of the front property.

The home's right wing focuses on sleeping quarters, with a luxurious master bedroom suite secluded at the rear of the plan. A graceful double-door entry introduces the suite, which boasts plenty of space for a sitting area and another set of double doors to the rear porch. The master bath, with its own linen closet, spa tub, and two vanities with sinks, allows access to the suite's walk-in closet. Two additional bedrooms, one of which can be used as a study, share a bath with a double vanity. ✿

Above: Bright trim and wall paneling help the foyer make an impact on visitors. The plan can be modified to include doors to the bedroom/study in place of the nook occupied by the cabinet.

Below: Beadboard and tile add texture to the master bath.

Also noteworthy is the kitchen, with its perfect blend of form and function.

Above: The well-designed kitchen has everything yet doesn't take up a lot of space.

Left: Opportunity for cozy private spaces—such as this one, in the master suite—exists throughout the home.

Below: The smallest of the bedrooms can be modified into a study.

The back porch sets
an attractive scene for seasonal living.

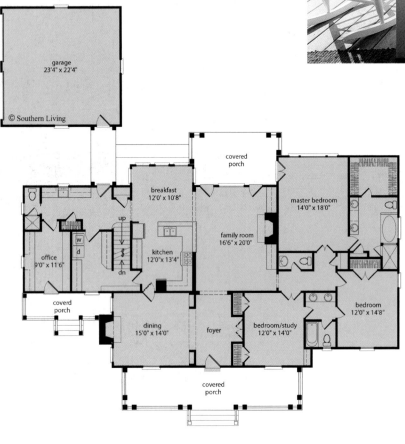

garage
23'4" x 22'4"

© Southern Living

covered
porch

breakfast
12'0" x 10'8"

up

office
9'0" x 11'6"

w
d

kitchen
12'0"x 13'4"

family room
16'6" x 20'0"

master bedroom
14'0" x 18'0"

dn

coverd
porch

dining
15'0" x 14'0"

foyer

bedroom/study
12'0" x 14'0"

bedroom
12'0" x 14'8"

covered
porch

optional bedroom
12'0" x 17'0"

dn

SAND MOUNTAIN

PLAN #HPK3700001

Designed by John Tee, Architect, for
The Progressive Farmer

Square Footage: 2,592

Bedrooms: 3

Bathrooms: 3 ½

Width: 80' - 0"

Depth: 78' - 0"

Foundation: Crawlspace

Price Code: L4

1–800–521–6797
eplans.com

Banning Court

2 *Bedrooms*	2 *Full Baths*

PLAN HPK3700002

Designed by Moser Design Group

Square Footage: 1,286

Width: 41' - 0"

Depth: 58' - 0"

Foundation: Crawlspace

Price Code: C1

1–800–850–1491
eplans.com

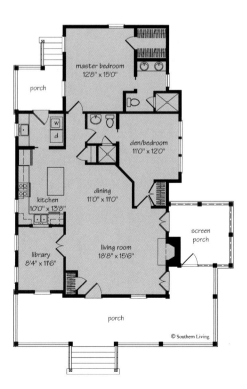

master bedroom
12'8" x 15'0"

porch

w
d

den/bedroom
11'0" x 12'0"

dining
11'0" x 11'0"

kitchen
10'0" x 13'8"

screen
porch

library
8'4" x 11'6"

living room
18'8" x 15'6"

porch

© Southern Living

Ashley River Cottage

PLAN #HPK3700003

Designed by Allison-Ramsey Architects, Inc.

First Floor: 1,093 sq. ft.

Second Floor: 512 sq. ft.

Total: 1,605 sq. ft.

Width: 33' - 0"

Depth: 51' - 0"

Foundation: Pier (same as Piling)

Price Code: C1

1-800-850-1491
eplans.com

3 *Bedrooms* 2 *Full Baths*

First Floor

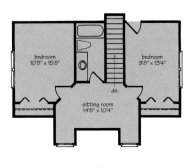

Second Floor

Ellsworth Cottage

| 3 Bedrooms | 2 Full Baths | 1 Half Bath |

PLAN #HPK3700004

Designed by Caldwell–Cline Architects and Designers

First Floor: 1,135 sq. ft.

Second Floor: 510 sq. ft.

Total: 1,645 sq. ft.

Width: 38' - 0"

Depth: 50' - 0"

Foundation: Unfinished Basement

Price Code: C1

1–800–850–1491
eplans.com

First Floor

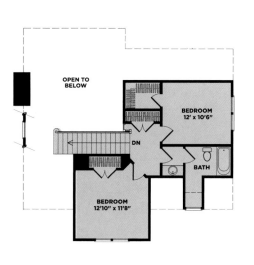

Second Floor

PLAN #HPK3700005

Designed by Caldwell–Cline Architects and Designers

First Floor: 1,215 sq. ft.

Second Floor: 500 sq. ft.

Total: 1,715 sq. ft.

Width: 65' - 0"

Depth: 46' - 0"

Foundation: Crawlspace, Slab, Unfinished Basement

Price Code: C1

1–800–850–1491

eplans.com

| 3 Bedrooms | 2 Full Baths | 1 Half Bath |

First Floor

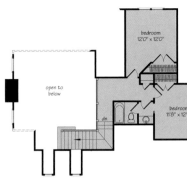

Second Floor

3 *Bedrooms* | 2 *Full Baths* | 1 *Half Bath*

PLAN #HPK3700006

Designed by Sullivan Design Company

First Floor: 1,154 sq. ft.

Second Floor: 621 sq. ft.

Total: 1,775 sq. ft.

Width: 44' - 0"

Depth: 49' - 0"

Foundation: Crawlspace

Price Code: C3

1–800–850–1491
eplans.com

First Floor

Second Floor

Buucksport Cottage

PLAN #HPK3700007

Designed by Moser Design Group

First Floor: 1,066 sq. ft.

Second Floor: 728 sq. ft.

Total: 1,794 sq. ft.

Width: 39' - 0"

Depth: 44' - 0"

Foundation: Crawlspace

Price Code: C1

1-800-850-1491
eplans.com

3 Bedrooms | *2 Full Baths* | *1 Half Bath*

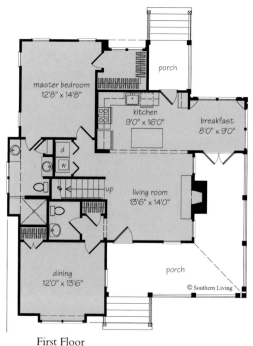

First Floor

Second Floor

© Southern Living

Gresham Creek Cottage

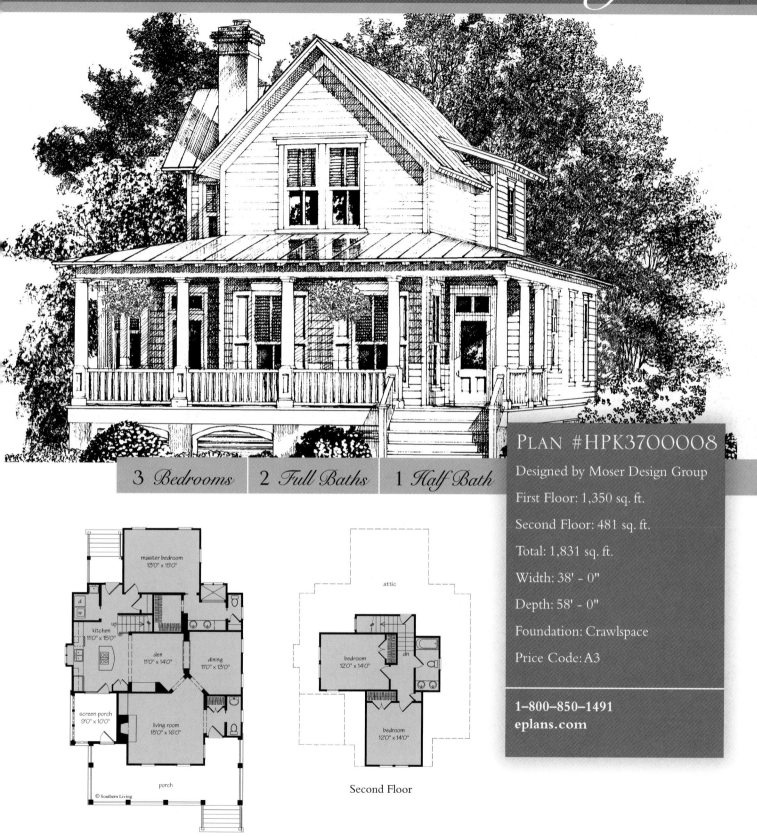

| 3 Bedrooms | 2 Full Baths | 1 Half Bath |

PLAN #HPK3700008

Designed by Moser Design Group

First Floor: 1,350 sq. ft.

Second Floor: 481 sq. ft.

Total: 1,831 sq. ft.

Width: 38' – 0"

Depth: 58' – 0"

Foundation: Crawlspace

Price Code: A3

1–800–850–1491
eplans.com

First Floor

Second Floor

1,938 square feet

Elizabeth's Place

PLAN #HPK3700009

Designed by Mitchell Ginn

First Floor: 983 sq. ft.

Second Floor: 955 sq. ft.

Total: 1,938 sq. ft.

Width: 70' - 0"

Depth: 51' - 0"

Foundation: Unfinished Basement

Price Code: C1

1–800–850–1491
eplans.com

3 *Bedrooms* | 2 *Full Baths* | 1 *Half Bath*

garage
23'4" x 21'4"

deck

eating
14'0" x 12'4"

family room
16'2" x 13'4"

screened porch
10'0" x 11'4"

© Southern Living

kitchen
14'0" x 11'8"

up

dn

foyer

dining
14'0" x 14'10"

porch

First Floor

bedroom
11'2" x 12'0"

bedroom
11'2" x 11'0"

dn

master bedroom
14'0" x 14'10"

Second Floor

Forestdale

3 *Bedrooms* | 3 *Full Baths*

PLAN #HPK3700010

Designed by Sullivan Design Company

Square Footage: 2,010

Width: 60' - 0"

Depth: 75' - 0"

Foundation: Crawlspace

Price Code: C3

1-800-850-1491
eplans.com

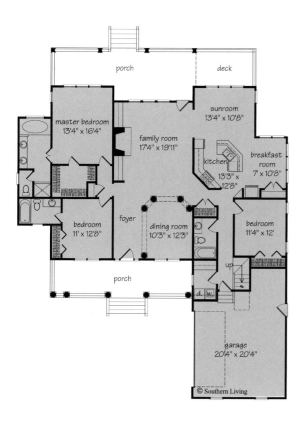

porch | deck

master bedroom
13'4" x 16'4"

family room
17'4" x 19'11"

sunroom
13'4" x 10'8"

kitchen
13'3" x 12'8"

breakfast room
7 x 10'8"

bedroom
11' x 12'8"

foyer

dining room
10'3" x 12'3"

bedroom
11'4" x 12'

porch

up

d. w.

garage
20'4" x 20'4"

© Southern Living

dn.

bonus room
13'8" x 20'4"

Cotton Hill Cottage

PLAN #HPK3700011

Designed by Bryan & Contreras, LLC

2 *Bedrooms*	3 *Full Baths*

First Floor: 1,161 sq. ft.

Second Floor: 922 sq. ft.

Total: 2,083 sq. ft.

Width: 36' - 4"

Depth: 46' - 6"

Foundation: Crawlspace

Price Code: C1

1–800–850–1491
eplans.com

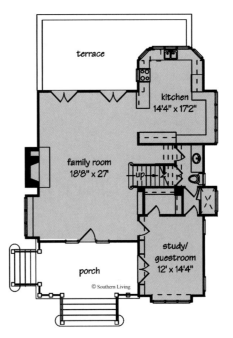

terrace

kitchen
14'4" x 17'2"

family room
18'8" x 27'

up

study/
guestroom
12' x 14'4"

porch

© Southern Living

First Floor

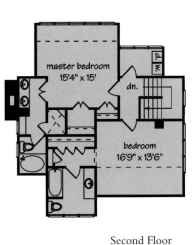

master bedroom
15'4" x 15'

dn.

bedroom
16'9" x 13'6"

Second Floor

Miss Maggie's House

3 *Bedrooms* | **2** *Full Baths* | **1** *Half Bath*

PLAN #HPK3700012

Designed by Mitchell Ginn

First Floor: 1,444 sq. ft.

Second Floor: 645 sq. ft.

Total: 2,089 sq. ft.

Width: 70' - 0"

Depth: 52' - 0"

Foundation: Unfinished Basement

Price Code: C1

1–800–850–1491
eplans.com

First Floor

Second Floor

Williams Bluff

PLAN #HPK3700013

Designed by Moser Design Group

First Floor: 1,534 sq. ft.

Second Floor: 610 sq. ft.

Total: 2,144 sq. ft.

Width: 40' - 0"

Depth: 67' - 0"

Foundation: Crawlspace

Price Code: C1

1–800–850–1491
eplans.com

3 *Bedrooms*   2 *Full Baths*   1 *Half Bath*

First Floor

Second Floor

Lowcountry Cottage

| 2 *Bedrooms* | 2 *Full Baths* | 1 *Half Bath* |

PLAN #HPK3700014

Designed by Moser Design Group for Cottage Living Magazine

First Floor: 1,631 sq. ft.

Second Floor: 517 sq. ft.

Total: 2,148 sq. ft.

Width: 39' - 0"

Depth: 73' - 0"

Foundation: Crawlspace

Price Code: C1

1-800-850-1491
eplans.com

Second Floor

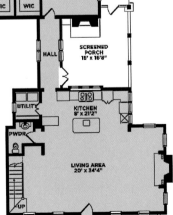

First Floor

Maple Hill

PLAN #HPK3700015

Designed by Sullivan Design Company

First Floor: 1,635 sq. ft.

Second Floor: 534 sq. ft.

Total: 2,169 sq. ft.

Width: 52' - 0"

Depth: 63' - 0"

Foundation: Crawlspace

Price Code: C1

1–800–850–1491
eplans.com

3 *Bedrooms* | 2 *Full Baths* | 1 *Half Bath*

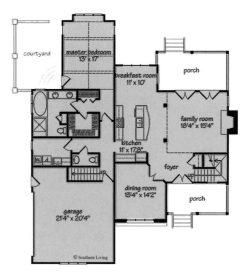

First Floor

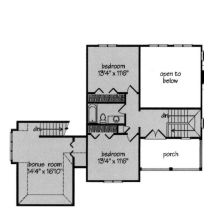

Second Floor

Aiken Ridge

3 *Bedrooms*   **3** *Full Baths*   **1** *Half Bath*

PLAN #HPK3700016

Designed by Moser Design Group

First Floor: 1,580 sq. ft.

Second Floor: 622 sq. ft.

Total: 2,202 sq. ft.

Width: 40' - 0"

Depth: 60' - 0"

Foundation: Crawlspace

Price Code: C3

1–800–850–1491
eplans.com

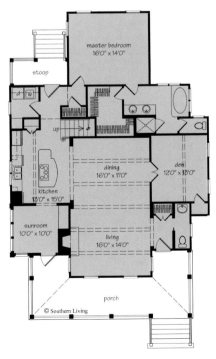

First Floor

Second Floor

New Rustic Oaks

PLAN #HPK3700017

Designed by John Tee, Architect

Square Footage: 2,208

Width: 80' - 0"

Depth: 48' - 0"

Foundation: Crawlspace

Price Code: C3

1–800–850–1491
eplans.com

| 2 *Bedrooms* | 2 *Full Baths* | 1 *Half Bath* |

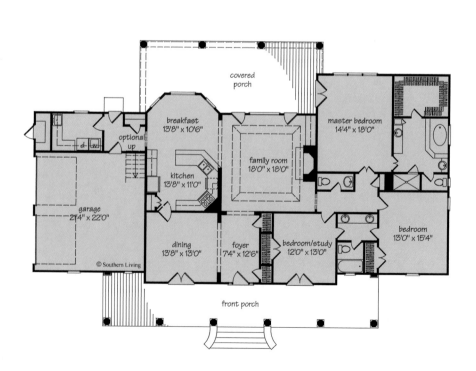

© Southern Living

garage
21'4" x 22'0"

breakfast
13'8" x 10'6"

optional up

kitchen
13'8" x 11'0"

family room
18'0" x 18'0"

covered porch

master bedroom
14'4" x 18'0"

dining
13'8" x 13'0"

foyer
7'4" x 12'6"

bedroom/study
12'0" x 13'0"

bedroom
13'0" x 15'4"

front porch

Bradley House

| 3 Bedrooms | 3 Full Baths | 1 Half Bath |

PLAN HPK3700018

Designed by Moser Design Group

First Floor: 1,412 sq. ft.

Second Floor: 806 sq. ft.

Total: 2,218 sq. ft.

Width: 44' - 0"

Depth: 51' - 0"

Foundation: Crawlspace

Price Code: C3

1-800-850-1491
eplans.com

First Floor

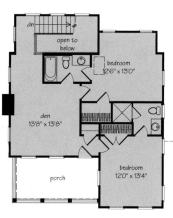

Second Floor

New Round Hill

PLAN #HPK3700019

Designed by John Tee, Architect

Square Footage: 2,242

Width: 76' - 0"

Depth: 78' - 0"

Foundation: Crawlspace

Price Code: C3

1–800–850–1491
eplans.com

2 *Bedrooms* | 2 *Full Baths* | 2 *Half Baths*

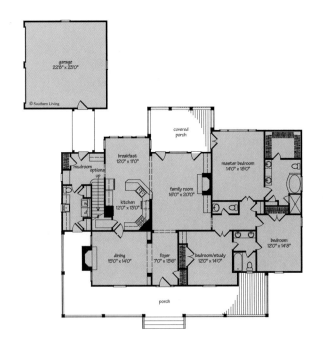

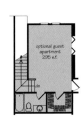

Amberview Way

3 *Bedrooms* | 2 *Full Baths*

PLAN #HPK3700020

Designed by Sullivan Design Company

First Floor: 1,953 sq. ft.

Second Floor: 336 sq. ft.

Total: 2,289 sq. ft.

Width: 61' - 0"

Depth: 55' - 0"

Foundation: Crawlspace

Price Code: C1

1–800–850–1491
eplans.com

First Floor

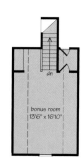

Second Floor

Angel Oak Point

PLAN #HPK3700021

Designed by Moser Design Group

First Floor: 1,462 sq. ft.

Second Floor: 837 sq. ft.

Total: 2,299 sq. ft.

Width: 33' - 0"

Depth: 71' - 0"

Foundation: Crawlspace

Price Code: C1

1–800–850–1491
eplans.com

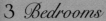

3 *Bedrooms* | 3 *Full Baths* | 1 *Half Bath*

First Floor

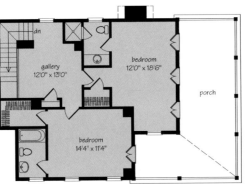

Second Floor

River View Cottage

2,315 square feet

3 *Bedrooms* | 2 *Full Baths* | 1 *Half Bath*

PLAN #HPK3700022

Designed by Looney Ricks Kiss Architects, Inc.

First Floor: 1,234 sq. ft.

Second Floor: 1,081 sq. ft.

Total: 2,315 sq. ft.

Width: 34' – 0"

Depth: 95' – 0"

Foundation: Crawlspace

Price Code: C3

1–800–850–1491
eplans.com

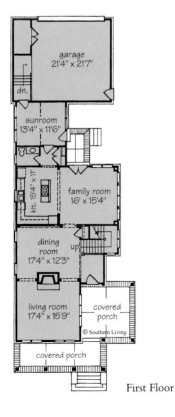

First Floor

- garage 21'4" x 21'7"
- dn.
- sunroom 13'4" x 11'6"
- kit. 15'4" x 11'
- family room 16' x 15'4"
- up
- dining room 17'4" x 12'3"
- living room 17'4" x 15'9"
- covered porch
- covered porch
- © Southern Living

Second Floor

- bedroom 11' x 14'4"
- bedroom 10' x 13'
- dn.
- master bedroom 17'4" x 15'9"
- covered porch

Franklin House

PLAN #HPK3700023

Designed by Mouzon Design

First Floor: 1,704 sq. ft.

Second Floor: 648 sq. ft.

Total: 2,352 sq. ft.

Width: 45' - 0"

Depth: 91' - 0"

Foundation: Crawlspace

Price Code: L4

1-800-850-1491
eplans.com

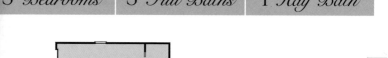

3 *Bedrooms* | 3 *Full Baths* | 1 *Half Bath*

First Floor

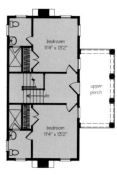

Second Floor

Winnsboro Heights

| 4 *Bedrooms* | 2 *Full Baths* | 1 *Half Bath* |

PLAN #HPK3700024

Designed by Moser Design Group

First Floor: 1,462 sq. ft.

Second Floor: 893 sq. ft.

Total: 2,355 sq. ft.

Width: 42' - 0"

Depth: 60' - 0"

Foundation: Crawlspace

Price Code: C1

1–800–850–1491
eplans.com

First Floor

Second Floor

Valensole

PLAN #HPK3700025

Designed by Sullivan Design Company

First Floor: 1,391 sq. ft.

Second Floor: 969 sq. ft.

Total: 2,360 sq. ft.

Width: 56' - 0"

Depth: 68' - 0"

Foundation: Crawlspace

Price Code: C3

1-800-850-1491
eplans.com

3 *Bedrooms*   2 *Full Baths*   1 *Half Bath*

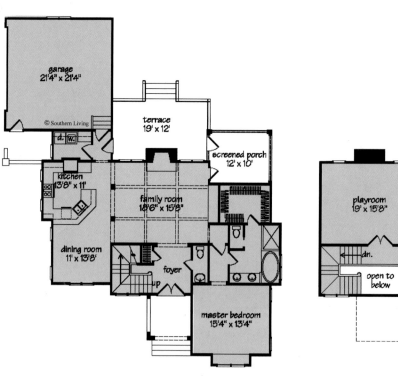

First Floor   Second Floor

Mabry Cottage

3 *Bedrooms*	2 *Full Baths*	1 *Half Bath*

PLAN #HPK3700026

Designed by Looney Ricks Kiss Architects, Inc. for Cottage Living Magazine

First Floor: 1,774 sq. ft.

Second Floor: 598 sq. ft.

Total: 2,372 sq. ft.

Width: 73' – 0"

Depth: 40' – 0"

Foundation: Slab

Price Code: C3

1–800–850–1491
eplans.com

First Floor

Second Floor

Peachtree Cottage

PLAN #HPK3700027

Designed by John Tee, Architect

Square Footage: 2,390

Width: 80' - 0"

Depth: 55' - 0"

Foundation: Crawlspace, Unfinished Basement

Price Code: C3

1-800-850-1491
eplans.com

3 Bedrooms | *2 Full Baths* | *1 Half Bath*

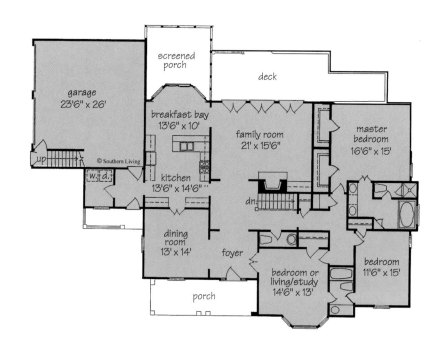

© Southern Living

garage 23'6" x 26'

screened porch

deck

breakfast bay 13'6" x 10'

family room 21' x 15'6"

master bedroom 16'6" x 15'

up

w.d.

kitchen 13'6" x 14'6"

dn.

dining room 13' x 14'

foyer

bedroom or living/study 14'6" x 13'

bedroom 11'6" x 15'

porch

Lakeside Cottage

| 3 *Bedrooms* | 2 *Full Baths* | 1 *Half Bath* |

PLAN #HPK3700028

Designed by William H. Phillips

Square Footage: 2,400

Width: 76' - 3"

Depth: 65' - 9"

Foundation: Crawlspace

Price Code: A4

1–800–850–1491
eplans.com

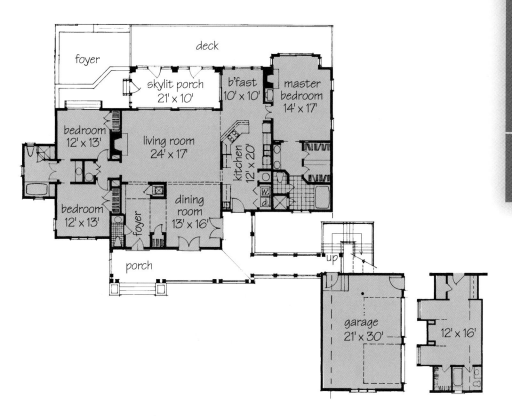

Pennington Point

PLAN #HPK3700029

Designed by Moser Design Group

First Floor: 1,764 sq. ft.

Second Floor: 637 sq. ft.

Total: 2,401 sq. ft.

Width: 49' – 0"

Depth: 80' – 0"

Foundation: Crawlspace

Price Code: C3

1–800–850–1491
eplans.com

3 *Bedrooms* | 2 *Full Baths* | 1 *Half Bath*

First Floor

Second Floor

| 3 *Bedrooms* | 2 *Full Baths* | 1 *Half Bath* |

PLAN #HPK3700030

Designed by John Tee, Architect

Square Footage: 2,404

Width: 70' - 0"

Depth: 63' - 0"

Foundation: Unfinished Basement

Price Code: L1

1–800–850–1491
eplans.com

porch

bedroom
13'0" x 12'0"

family room
21'4" x 17'4"

breakfast
11'8" x 11'0"

master bedroom
14'4" x 18'0"

kitchen
13'8" x 12'8"

bedroom
13'0" x 15'8"

foyer
6'8" x 16'0"

dining
12'0" x 15'4"

up

w

up

porch

garage
21'4" x 24'0"

© Southern Living

Montereau

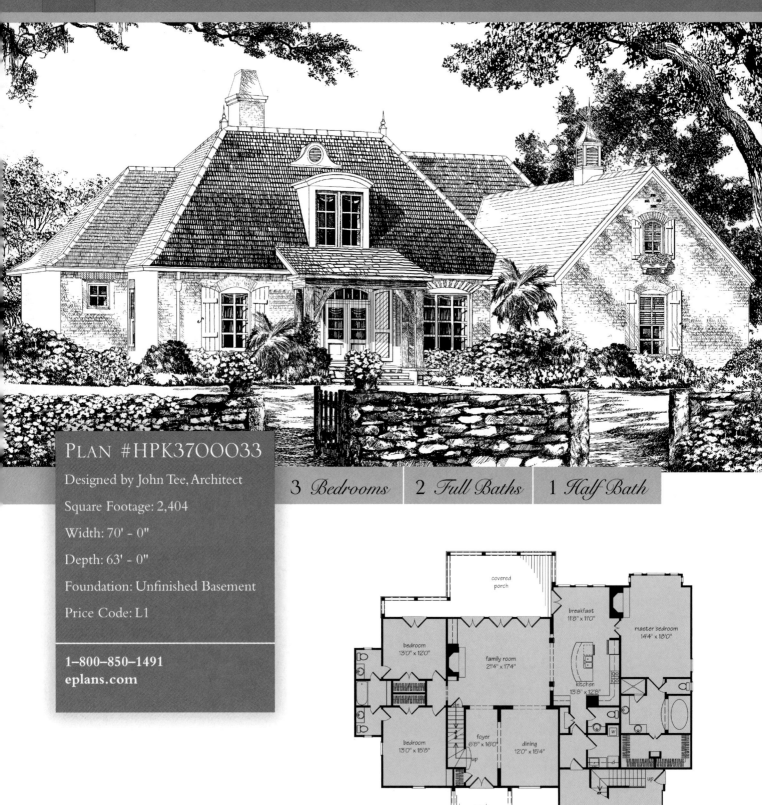

PLAN #HPK3700033

Designed by John Tee, Architect

Square Footage: 2,404

Width: 70' - 0"

Depth: 63' - 0"

Foundation: Unfinished Basement

Price Code: L1

1–800–850–1491
eplans.com

3 *Bedrooms* | 2 *Full Baths* | 1 *Half Bath*

covered porch

breakfast 11'8" x 11'0"

master bedroom 14'4" x 18'0"

bedroom 13'0" x 12'0"

family room 21'4" x 17'4"

kitchen 13'8" x 12'8"

bedroom 13'0" x 15'8"

foyer 6'8" x 16'0"

dining 12'0" x 15'4"

up

w

porch

garage 21'4" x 24'0"

© Southern Living

The Park

| 4 Bedrooms | 2 Full Baths | 1 Half Bath |

PLAN #HPK3700032

Designed by Gary/Ragsdale, Inc.

Square Footage: 2,420

Width: 60' - 0"

Depth: 63' - 0"

Foundation: Crawlspace

Price Code: C3

1-800-850-1491
eplans.com

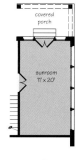

Optional Layout

Beaumont

PLAN #HPK3700031

Designed by Gary/Ragsdale, Inc.

Square Footage: 2,420

Width: 60' - 0"

Depth: 63' - 0"

Foundation: Crawlspace

Price Code: C3

1–800–850–1491
eplans.com

| 4 Bedrooms | 2 Full Baths | 1 Half Bath |

Optional Layout

Whitestone

| 3 *Bedrooms* | 2 *Full Baths* | 1 *Half Bath* |

PLAN #HPK3700034

Designed by Bryan & Contreras, LLC

First Floor: 1,835 sq. ft.

Second Floor: 595 sq. ft.

Total: 2,430 sq. ft.

Width: 67' - 0"

Depth: 68' - 0"

Foundation: Unfinished Basement

Price Code: C3

1-800-850-1491
eplans.com

First Floor

Second Floor

Westbury Park

PLAN #HPK3700035

Designed by Moser Design Group

First Floor: 1,905 sq. ft.

Second Floor: 552 sq. ft.

Total: 2,457 sq. ft.

Width: 66' - 2"

Depth: 52' - 3"

Foundation: Crawlspace

Price Code: C3

1-800-850-1491

eplans.com

3 *Bedrooms* | 2 *Full Baths* | 1 *Half Bath*

First Floor

Second Floor

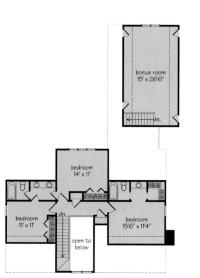

Stonebridge Cottage

4 Bedrooms | **3 Full Baths** | **1 Half Bath**

PLAN #HPK3700036

Designed by Sullivan Design Company

First Floor: 1,696 sq. ft.

Second Floor: 788 sq. ft.

Total: 2,484 sq. ft.

Width: 63' - 0"

Depth: 77' - 0"

Foundation: Crawlspace

Price Code: C3

1–800–850–1491
eplans.com

First Floor

Second Floor

garage 23' x 23'
deck
dining room 15'8" x 13'8"
kitchen 13'8" x 14'
master bedroom 13'4" x 17'
foyer
living room 18'10" x 18'4"
porch
© Southern Living

bonus room 15' x 26'6"
bedroom 14' x 11'
bedroom 11' x 11'
bedroom 15'6" x 11'4"
open to below

Moore's Creek

PLAN #HPK3700037

Designed by John Tee, Architect

Square Footage: 2,540

Width: 84' - 0"

Depth: 53' - 0"

Foundation: Unfinished Basement

Price Code: C3

1–800–850–1491
eplans.com

| 3 *Bedrooms* | 2 *Full Baths* | 2 *Half Baths* |

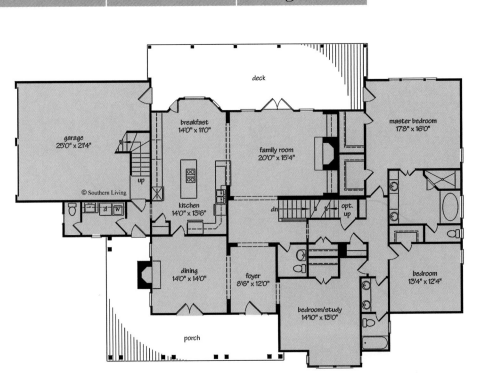

deck

garage
25'0" x 21'4"

breakfast
14'0" x 11'0"

family room
20'0" x 15'4"

master bedroom
17'8" x 16'0"

up

© Southern Living

kitchen
14'0" x 13'6"

dn

opt.
up

dining
14'0" x 14'0"

foyer
8'6" x 12'0"

bedroom
13'4" x 12'4"

bedroom/study
14'10" x 13'0"

porch

Belhaven Place

| 3 Bedrooms | 3 Full Baths | 1 Half Bath |

First Floor

Second Floor

PLAN #HPK3700038

Designed by Looney Ricks Kiss Architects, Inc.

First Floor: 1,989 sq. ft.

Second Floor: 617 sq. ft.

Total: 2,576 sq. ft.

Width: 62' - 0"

Depth: 82' - 0"

Foundation: Slab

Price Code: C3

1–800–850–1491
eplans.com

Pine Hill Cottage

PLAN #HPK3700039

Designed by Bryan & Contreras, LLC

First Floor: 1,938 sq. ft.

Second Floor: 651 sq. ft.

Total: 2,589 sq. ft.

Width: 53' - 0"

Depth: 57' - 0"

Foundation: Unfinished Basement

Price Code: C3

1-800-850-1491
eplans.com

4 *Bedrooms*   **3** *Full Baths*

First Floor

Second Floor

covered porch

© Southern Living

master bedroom
14' x 15'

family room
24' x 21'

up

kitchen
11'9" x 17'6"

bedroom
11' x 14'4"

foyer

dining room
11'8" x 14'4"

porch

dn.

storage

bedroom
12' x 16'2"

bedroom
12' x 16'2"

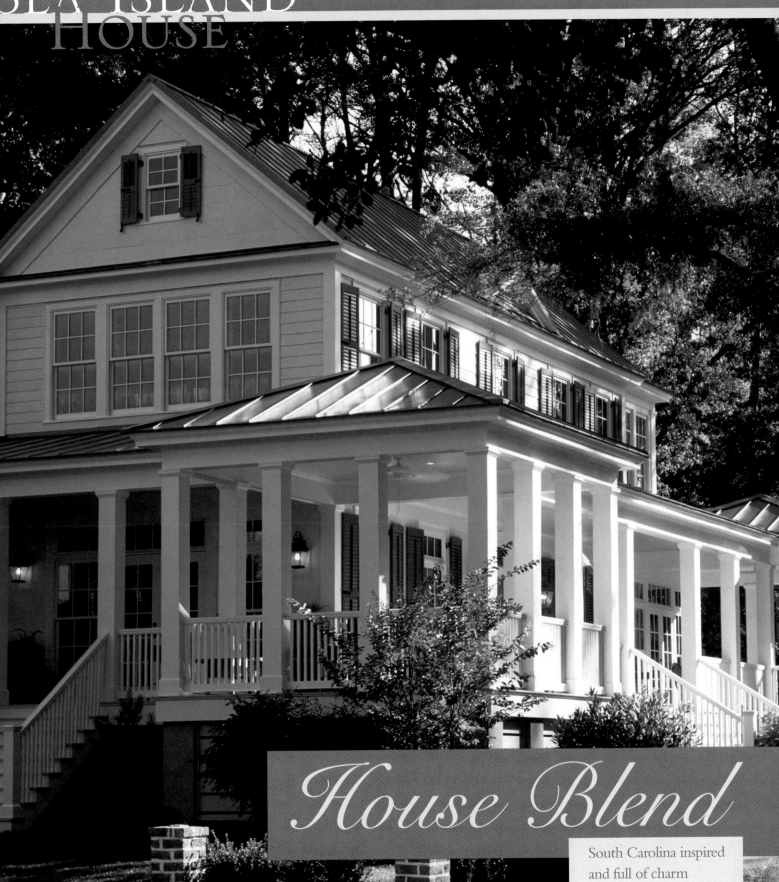

SEA ISLAND
HOUSE

House Blend

South Carolina inspired
and full of charm

SEA ISLAND HOUSE

The color scheme echoes that of the exterior, creating continuity from indoors to out.

A lowcountry home,

with an expansive wraparound porch and a spacious eat–in kitchen…. A design with crisp white siding topped by a metal roof…. A dignified traditional with shutters and a paneled front door…. In all these details, the Sea Island House embodies a style full of history and tradition.

While Sea Island House's simple yet striking facade honors the past, it also provides for today's comforts with three generously sized bedrooms, four full baths, and plenty of living space. The house plan embraces the outdoors as well; all first-floor living areas open to the wraparound porch, and the kitchen accesses a cozy side porch. Outdoor sitting and dining areas, furnished with casual yet classic wicker, allow family and guests to enjoy the hospitable southern climate.

Opposite Left: Sidelights and a transom distinguish the formal entry.

Opposite Right: A deep porch shades the home's sunnier exposures, keeping the home well-lit and cool.

Below Left: The free-flowing living room and dining room provide a unified gathering area.

Below: A side porch entry services the traditional country kitchen.

Each sun-filled bedroom is a full suite.

Sea Island House also welcomes modern conveniences. According to David Bryant, project manager at Historical Concepts, the home features durable materials on the exterior and porches. "It's got that old feel, but it's a maintenance-free building," says Bryant. He also notes that the living spaces feature standard, off-the-shelf moldings. Although working with custom moldings can be enjoyable, designing rooms based on standard moldings suited the needs of the designer and client.

The first-floor rooms display great versatility, flowing from formal to informal spaces as easily as they move between indoors and outdoors. A large, open area divides nicely into the living and dining rooms, which are lit by tall windows and warmed by fireplaces. The family room, fully open to the island kitchen, offers space for more relaxed gatherings as well as easy access to the outdoor sitting area. Next to the kitchen, a media room—with two walk-in closets and two wall closets—can serve as a computer center, home office, or family recreation room. On the opposite side of the first floor is space for

a study—here it serves as a radiant sunroom, with French doors allowing plenty of natural illumination. (The study can also function as a fourth bedroom, if desired.) A full bath, easily accessible to guests, completes the first floor.

An elegant staircase just beyond the foyer leads upstairs, where the rooms are also arranged for comfort and convenience. All three bedrooms include full private baths; the bath in the master suite is especially luxurious, with two vanities, a walk-in shower, and an elegant claw-foot tub positioned near a boxed window to take full advantage of natural light. A centrally located laundry room provides cabinets, counters, and a storage closet.

The design team always "makes a strong effort to get the interior to relate to the exterior," says Bryant. Their efforts are evident here. Various shades of blue, from soothingly soft in the bedrooms to dramatic and bold downstairs, highlight the smooth white walls and natural wood floors and panels found throughout the house. The color scheme echoes that of the exterior, creating continuity from indoors to out. ❀

SEA ISLAND HOUSE

PLAN #HPK3700040

Designed by Historical Concepts, LLC, for Coastal Living Magazine

First Floor: 1,584 sq. ft.

Second Floor: 1,154 sq. ft.

Total: 2,738 sq. ft.

Bedrooms: 3

Bathrooms: 4

Width: 69' - 0"

Depth: 45' - 0"

Foundation: Crawlspace

Price Code: SQ5

1–800–521–6797
eplans.com

First Floor

study
13'11" x 11'

media room
9' x 9'

kitchen
13' x 12'6"

porch

living room

38' x 17'6"

dining room

keeping room
13' x 17'6"

up

entry

porch

porch

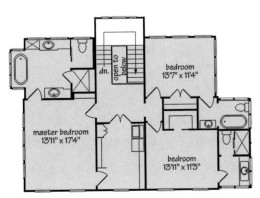

Second Floor

master bedroom
13'11" x 17'4"

bedroom
13'7" x 11'4"

bedroom
13'11" x 11'3"

dn.

open to below

Above Left: The keeping room is a casual family area at the side of the home.

Above Right: Full-height windows and French doors surround the very scenic living room.

Bluff Haven

PLAN #HPK3700161

Designed by Bryan & Contreras, LLC

First Floor: 1,389 sq. ft.

Second Floor: 1,213 sq. ft.

Total: 2,602 sq. ft.

Width: 48' - 0"

Depth: 46' - 0"

Foundation: Crawlspace

Price Code: C1

1–800–850–1491
eplans.com

3 *Bedrooms* | **4** *Full Baths*

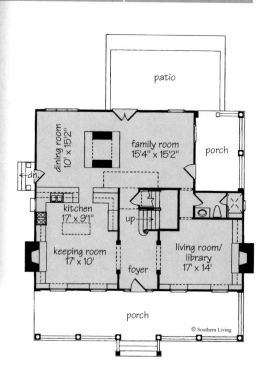

First Floor

Second Floor

Poppy Point

| 3 *Bedrooms* | 2 *Full Baths* | 1 *Half Bath* |

PLAN #HPK3700071

Designed by Gary/Ragsdale, Inc.

Square Footage: 2,604

Bonus Space: 350 sq. ft.

Width: 49' - 0"

Depth: 89' - 0"

Foundation: Slab

Price Code: C3

1-800-850-1491
eplans.com

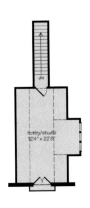

Cottage of the Year

PLAN #HPK3700042

Designed by Moser Design Group
for Coastal Living magazine

First Floor: 2,028 sq. ft.

Second Floor: 584 sq. ft.

Total: 2,612 sq. ft.

Width: 65' – 0"

Depth: 77' – 0"

Foundation: Pier (same as Piling)

Price Code: L4

1–800–850–1491
eplans.com

| 4 Bedrooms | 3 Full Baths | 1 Half Bath |

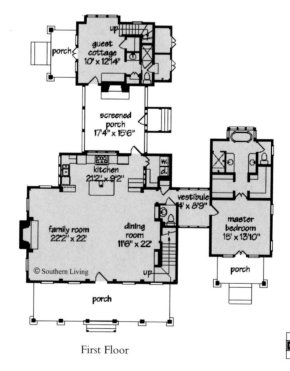

guest cottage 10' x 12'4"

porch

screened porch 17'4" x 15'6"

kitchen 21'2" x 9'2"

w.d.

vestibule 4' x 8'9"

master bedroom 15' x 13'10"

family room 22'2" x 22'

dining room 11'6" x 22'

porch

up

porch

© Southern Living

First Floor

open to below

guest cottage loft

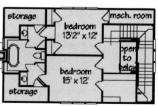

storage

bedroom 13'2" x 12'

mech. room

open to below

bedroom 15' x 12'

storage

Second Floor

New Lynwood

| 3 Bedrooms | 2 Full Baths | 2 Half Baths |

PLAN #HPK3700054

Designed by John Tee, Architect

Square Footage: 2,620

Width: 72' - 0"

Depth: 70' - 0"

Foundation: Unfinished Basement

Price Code: C3

1–800–850–1491
eplans.com

New Meadowlark

PLAN #HPK3700043

Designed by John Tee, Architect

Square Footage: 2,628

Width: 71' - 0"

Depth: 60' - 0"

Foundation: Crawlspace

Price Code: C3

1-800-850-1491
eplans.com

3 *Bedrooms* | 2 *Full Baths* | 1 *Half Bath*

Poplar Creek Cottage

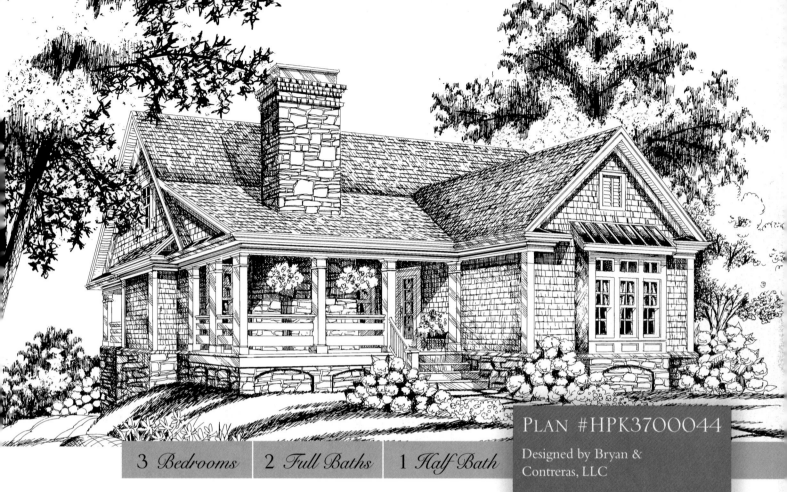

| 3 Bedrooms | 2 Full Baths | 1 Half Bath |

PLAN #HPK3700044

Designed by Bryan & Contreras, LLC

First Floor: 2,026 sq. ft.

Second Floor: 602 sq. ft.

Total: 2,628 sq. ft.

Width: 46' - 0"

Depth: 82' - 0"

Foundation: Unfinished Basement

Price Code: C3

1–800–850–1491
eplans.com

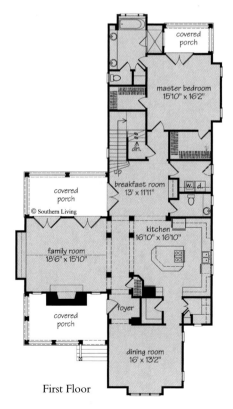

covered porch

master bedroom
15'10" x 16'2"

breakfast room
13' x 11'11"

covered porch

© Southern Living

family room
18'6" x 15'10"

kitchen
16'10" x 16'10"

covered porch

foyer

dining room
16' x 13'2"

First Floor

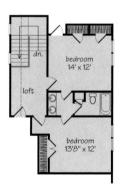

bedroom
14' x 12'

loft

bedroom
13'8" x 12'

Second Floor

Mandeville Place

PLAN #HPK3700045

Designed by John Tee, Architect

Square Footage: 2,638

Width: 78' - 0"

Depth: 51' - 0"

Foundation: Crawlspace

Price Code: C3

1–800–850–1491
eplans.com

| 2 *Bedrooms* | 2 *Full Baths* | 1 *Half Bath* |

covered porch

breakfast
13'4" x 11'4"

family room
20'8" x 15'0"

master bedroom
18'0" x 18'0"

w
d

up

kitchen
13'4" x 13'2"

gallery

master bath

garage
23'0" x 20'4"

stair can go up or down

dining
13'4" x 14'0"

foyer

© Southern Living

bedroom/study
13'4" x 14'10"

bedroom
12'10" x 12'2"

porch

3 *Bedrooms* | 2 *Full Baths* | 2 *Half Baths*

PLAN #HPK3700046

Designed by John Tee, Architect

Square Footage: 2,638

Width: 78' - 0"

Depth: 53' - 0"

Foundation: Crawlspace

Price Code: C1

1–800–850–1491
eplans.com

Spring Lake Cottage

Rear Perspective

PLAN #HPK3700047

Designed by Mouzon Design

First Floor: 1,978 sq. ft.

Second Floor: 661 sq. ft.

Total: 2,639 sq. ft.

Width: 82' - 0"

Depth: 64' - 0"

Foundation: Unfinished Basement

Price Code: L4

3 Bedrooms | **2** Full Baths | **1** Half Bath

1–800–850–1491
eplans.com

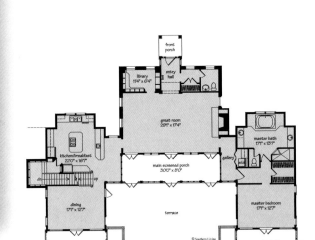

First Floor

Second Floor

Alta Vista

| 3 Bedrooms | 2 Full Baths | 1 Half Bath |

PLAN #HPK3700048

Designed by Mouzon Design for Biltmore Estate

First Floor: 1,938 sq. ft.

Second Floor: 866 sq. ft.

Total: 2,645 sq. ft.

Width: 71' - 0"

Depth: 75' - 0"

Foundation: Crawlspace

Price Code: L4

1-800-850-1491
eplans.com

First Floor

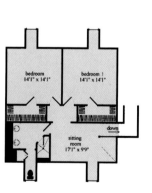

Second Floor

BILTMORE™
For Your Home

Overton Place

PLAN #HPK3700049

Designed by Sullivan Design Company

4 Bedrooms | **4 Full Baths**

First Floor: 1,733 sq. ft.

Second Floor: 919 sq. ft.

Total: 2,652 sq. ft.

Width: 66' - 0"

Depth: 54' - 0"

Foundation: Crawlspace

Price Code: C3

1–800–850–1491
eplans.com

First Floor

Second Floor

Turnball Park

3 *Bedrooms*	2 *Full Baths*	1 *Half Bath*

PLAN #HPK3700050

Designed by Moser Design Group

First Floor: 1,537 sq. ft.

Second Floor: 1,123 sq. ft.

Total: 2,660 sq. ft.

Width: 40' - 0"

Depth: 70' - 0"

Foundation: Crawlspace

Price Code: C3

1–800–850–1491
eplans.com

First Floor

Second Floor

Elderberry Place

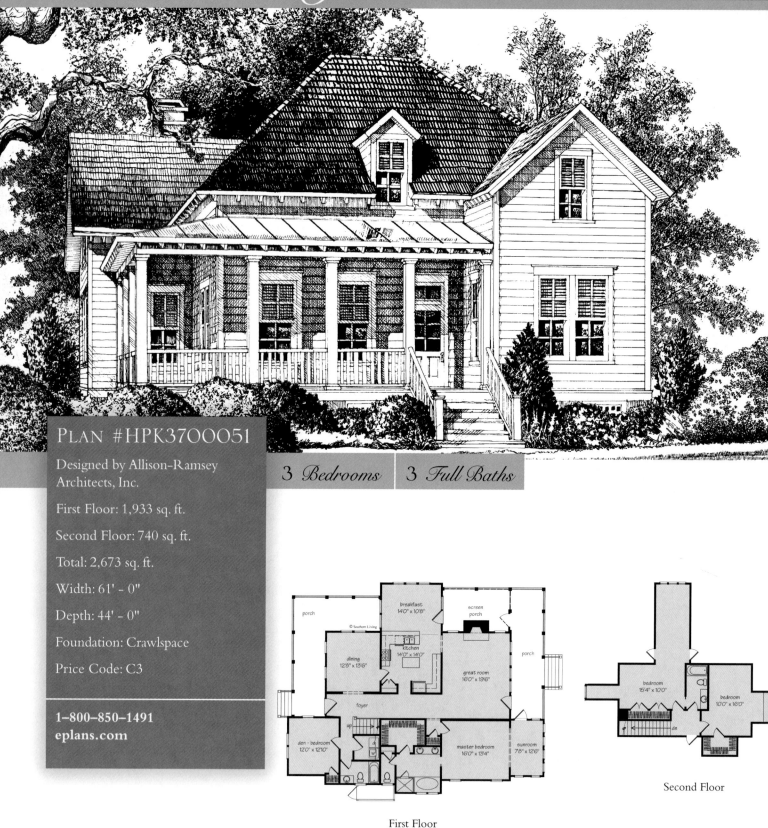

PLAN #HPK3700051

Designed by Allison-Ramsey Architects, Inc.

First Floor: 1,933 sq. ft.

Second Floor: 740 sq. ft.

Total: 2,673 sq. ft.

Width: 61' – 0"

Depth: 44' – 0"

Foundation: Crawlspace

Price Code: C3

1–800–850–1491
eplans.com

3 Bedrooms   *3 Full Baths*

porch

breakfast
14'0" x 10'8"

screen
porch

© Southern Living

dining
12'8" x 13'6"

kitchen
14'0" x 14'0"

porch

great room
16'0" x 19'6"

foyer

up

den - bedroom
12'0" x 12'10"

master bedroom
16'0" x 13'4"

sunroom
7'8" x 12'6"

First Floor

bedroom
15'4" x 10'0"

bedroom
10'0" x 18'0"

dn

Second Floor

3 *Bedrooms* **2** *Full Baths* **1** *Half Bath*

PLAN #HPK3700052

Designed by Gary/Ragsdale, Inc.

First Floor: 2,155 sq. ft.

Second Floor: 520 sq. ft.

Total: 2,675 sq. ft.

Width: 51' - 0"

Depth: 89' - 0"

Foundation: Crawlspace

Price Code: C3

1–800–850–1491
eplans.com

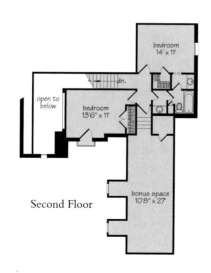

First Floor

- optional sunroom 16' x 12'
- family room 18' x 18'8"
- master bedroom 15' x 18'
- porch
- breakfast room 10'2" x 9'2"
- kitchen 18' x 13'10"
- study 11' x 11'4"
- up
- foyer
- dining room 16' x 11'
- w. d.
- porch
- garage 20'4" x 26'
- © Southern Living

Second Floor

- bedroom 14' x 11'
- open to below
- dn.
- bedroom 13'6" x 11'
- bonus space 10'8" x 27'

Grissom Trail
Southern Living Style

PLAN #HPK3700053

Designed by Moser Design Group

First Floor: 1,554 sq. ft.

Second Floor: 1,123 sq. ft.

Total: 2,677 sq. ft.

Width: 40' - 0"

Depth: 67' - 0"

Foundation: Crawlspace

Price Code: C1

1-800-850-1491
eplans.com

4 Bedrooms | *3 Full Baths* | *1 Half Bath*

First Floor

Second Floor

McKenzie Cottage

3 Bedrooms | **4 Full Baths**

PLAN #HPK3700060

Designed by Bryan & Contreras, LLC

First Floor: 1,930 sq. ft.

Second Floor: 820 sq. ft.

Total: 2,750 sq. ft.

Width: 60' - 0"

Depth: 46' - 0"

Foundation: Crawlspace

Price Code: C1

1-800-850-1491
eplans.com

First Floor

Second Floor

New Cooper's Bluff

PLAN #HPK3700057

Designed by John Tee, Architect

Square Footage: 2,824

Width: 73' - 0"

Depth: 63' - 0"

Foundation: Unfinished Basement

Price Code: L1

1–800–850–1491

eplans.com

3 *Bedrooms* | 3 *Full Baths* | 1 *Half Bath*

© Southern Living

Kilburne

4 *Bedrooms* | 3 *Full Baths* | 1 *Half Bath*

PLAN #HPK3700162

Designed by Frusterio & Associates

First Floor: 1,887 sq. ft.

Second Floor: 952 sq. ft.

Total: 2,839 sq. ft.

Width: 54' - 0"

Depth: 46' - 0"

Foundation: Unfinished Basement

Price Code: C3

1-800-850-1491
eplans.com

First Floor

Second Floor

2,858 square feet

New Holly Springs

PLAN #HPK3700058

Designed by John Tee, Architect

First Floor: 2,058 sq. ft.

Second Floor: 800 sq. ft.

Total: 2,858 sq. ft.

Width: 66' - 0"

Depth: 66' - 0"

Foundation: Crawlspace

Price Code: L1

1–800–850–1491
eplans.com

5 *Bedrooms* | 4 *Full Baths* | 1 *Half Bath*

First Floor

Second Floor

New Shannon

| 4 Bedrooms | 3 Full Baths | 2 Half Baths |

PLAN #HPK3700059

Designed by John Tee, Architect

First Floor: 1,952 sq. ft.

Second Floor: 912 sq. ft.

Total: 2,864 sq. ft.

Width: 66' - 0"

Depth: 50' - 0"

Foundation: Crawlspace

Price Code: C3

1-800-850-1491
eplans.com

First Floor

Second Floor

Northridge

PLAN #HPK3700061

Designed by Sullivan Design Company

First Floor: 1,969 sq. ft.

Second Floor: 907 sq. ft.

Total: 2,876 sq. ft.

Width: 70' - 0"

Depth: 79' - 0"

Foundation: Crawlspace

Price Code: C3

1–800–850–1491
eplans.com

4 *Bedrooms*   3 *Full Baths*   1 *Half Bath*

First Floor

Second Floor

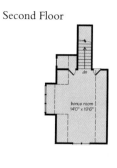

Iberville

3 *Bedrooms* | 3 *Full Baths* | 1 *Half Bath*

PLAN #HPK3700063

Designed by John Tee, Architect

Square Footage: 2,880

Width: 75' - 0"

Depth: 69' - 0"

Foundation: Unfinished Basement

Price Code: L1

1–800–850–1491

eplans.com

covered back porch

breakfast
14'0" x 10'0"

bedroom
14'4" x 12'0"

kitchen
14'0" x 13'0"

family room
20'6" x 15'4"

master bedroom
15'4" x 19'0"

bedroom
11'6" x 11'4"

w
d

dining
14'0" x 14'0"

foyer
6'10 x 13'8

living
13'0" x 14'0"

up

garage
20'10" x 21'4"

covered porch

© Southern Living

Fairfield Place

PLAN #HPK3700064

Designed by Sullivan Design Company

First Floor: 1,156 sq. ft.

Second Floor: 1,733 sq. ft.

Total: 2,889 sq. ft.

Width: 40' – 0"

Depth: 77' – 0"

Foundation: Crawlspace

Price Code: C3

1–800–850–1491
eplans.com

4 *Bedrooms* | 3 *Full Baths* | 1 *Half Bath*

First Floor

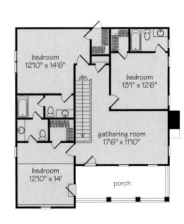

Second Floor

Wesley

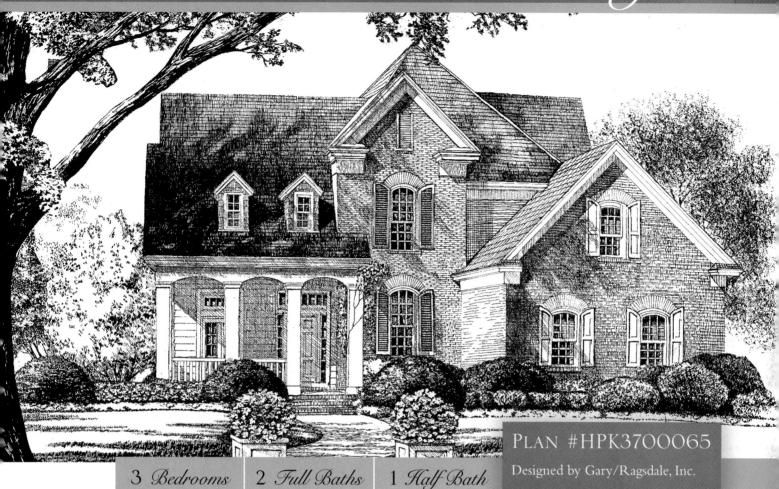

| 3 *Bedrooms* | 2 *Full Baths* | 1 *Half Bath* |

PLAN #HPK3700065

Designed by Gary/Ragsdale, Inc.

First Floor: 2,375 sq. ft.

Second Floor: 520 sq. ft.

Total: 2,895 sq. ft.

Width: 51' - 0"

Depth: 89' - 0"

Foundation: Crawlspace

Price Code: C3

1-800-850-1491
eplans.com

First Floor

master bedroom
18' x 15'

master bath

garage
26' x 20'4"

sun room
12' x 16'

family room
18'4" x 18'

kitchen
13'10" x 17'4"

dining room
11' x 16'

porch

up

entry

porch

breakfast
12'2" x 9'2"

study
11'4" x 11'

Second Floor

bedroom
11' x 14'6"

attic
26' x 10'8"

up

bedroom
11' x 13'8"

open to below

River Bend Farmhouse

PLAN #HPK3700067

Designed by Mouzon Design

First Floor: 1,984 sq. ft.

Second Floor: 926 sq. ft.

Total: 2,910 sq. ft.

Width: 82' – 0"

Depth: 58' – 0"

Foundation: Crawlspace

Price Code: L4

1–800–850–1491
eplans.com

4 *Bedrooms* 3 *Full Baths* 1 *Half Bath*

First Floor

Second Floor

New Brookhaven

3 *Bedrooms* | 2 *Full Baths* | 2 *Half Baths*

PLAN #HPK3700068

Designed by John Tee, Architect

Square Footage: 2,920

Width: 79' – 0"

Depth: 64' – 0"

Foundation: Unfinished Basement

Price Code: C3

1–800–850–1491
eplans.com

master bedroom
16'0" x 18'0"

covered
back porch

family dining
17'0" x 8'2"

kitchen
8'6" x 17'0"

family room
19'4" x 15'0"

keeping room
17'0" x 14'4"

bedroom
14'0" x 11'8"

bedroom/study
12'4" x 11'0"

foyer
7'0" x 15'4"

dining room
12'0" x 15'4"

up

porch

garage
21'4" x 21'0"

© Southern Living

Arden Gate

PLAN #HPK3700062

Designed by Mouzon Design for Biltmore Estate

3 Bedrooms | **4 Full Baths**

First Floor: 2,179 sq. ft.

Second Floor: 743 sq. ft.

Total: 2,922 sq. ft.

Width: 61' - 0"

Depth: 89' - 0"

Foundation: Crawlspace

Price Code: L2

1–800–850–1491
eplans.com

First Floor

Second Floor

BILTMORE™
For Your Home

Allendale

| 3 *Bedrooms* | 3 *Full Baths* | 1 *Half Bath* |

PLAN #HPK3700069

Designed by John Tee, Architect

First Floor: 2,053 sq. ft.

Second Floor: 872 sq. ft.

Total: 2,925 sq. ft.

Width: 58' - 0"

Depth: 69' - 0"

Foundation: Crawlspace

Price Code: L1

1-800-850-1491
eplans.com

First Floor

Second Floor

2,932 square feet

Louisiana Garden Cottage

PLAN #HPK3700066

Designed by John Tee, Architect

First Floor: 1,949 sq. ft.

Second Floor: 983 sq. ft.

Total: 2,932 sq. ft.

Width: 76' - 0"

Depth: 59' - 0"

Foundation: Crawlspace

Price Code: C3

1–800–850–1491
eplans.com

3 Bedrooms | *2 Full Baths* | *1 Half Bath*

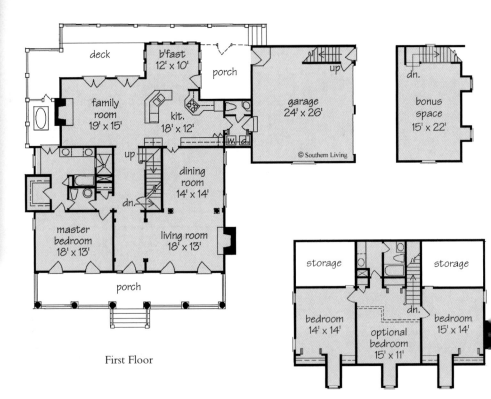

First Floor

Second Floor

Cumberland

| 3 *Bedrooms* | 2 *Full Baths* | 1 *Half Bath* |

PLAN #HPK3700070

Designed by John Tee, Architect

First Floor: 1,949 sq. ft.

Second Floor: 983 sq. ft.

Total: 2,932 sq. ft.

Width: 76' - 0"

Depth: 59' - 0"

Foundation: Crawlspace

Price Code: C3

1–800–850–1491
eplans.com

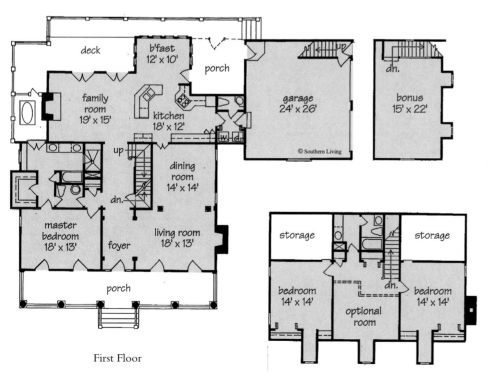

First Floor

Second Floor

Bedford Cottage

PLAN #HPK3700163

Designed by Looney Ricks Kiss Architects, Inc. for Cottage Living Magazine

First Floor: 1,589 sq. ft.

Second Floor: 1,362 sq. ft.

Total: 2,951 sq. ft.

Width: 58' - 0"

Depth: 77' - 0"

Foundation: Crawlspace

Price Code: L1

1–800–850–1491
eplans.com

3 *Bedrooms* | 2 *Full Baths* | 1 *Half Bath*

First Floor

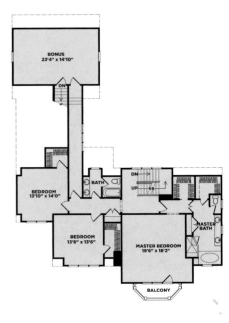

Second Floor

The Juliette

2,997 square feet

| 3 Bedrooms | 2 Full Baths | 1 Half Bath |

PLAN #HPK3700072

Designed by Bryan & Contreras, LLC

First Floor: 2,315 sq. ft.

Second Floor: 682 sq. ft.

Total: 2,997 sq. ft.

Width: 96' - 0"

Depth: 63' - 0"

Foundation: Unfinished Basement

Price Code: L1

1–800–850–1491
eplans.com

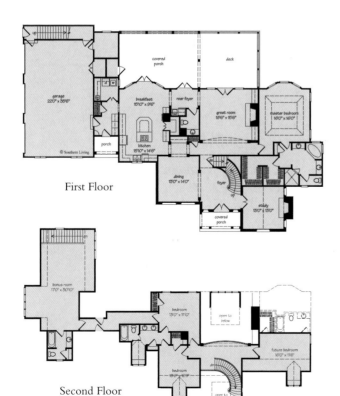

First Floor

Second Floor

Chestnut Hill

PLAN #HPK3700073

Designed by John Tee, Architect

First Floor: 1,934 sq. ft.

Second Floor: 1,064 sq. ft.

Total: 2,998 sq. ft.

Width: 81' - 0"

Depth: 81' - 0"

Foundation: Unfinished Basement

Price Code: L4

1–800–850–1491
eplans.com

3 Bedrooms | *3 Full Baths* | *1 Half Bath*

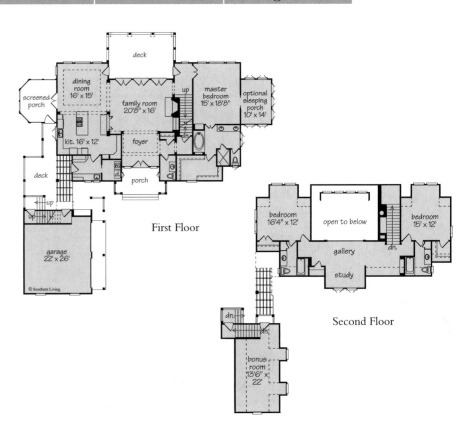

First Floor

Second Floor

POPLAR GROVE

Grand Tradition

A larger plan that delivers equal
parts style and convenience

POPLAR GROVE

Previous Page: The rear of the home embraces the outdoors.

Above: Furniture-style vanities complement the relaxing spa tub.

Right: Outdoor spaces are just steps away from indoor gathering rooms.

Below: Bedrooms are comfortably proportioned and full of charm.

At first glance,

Poplar Grove appears to be a simple yet sweet traditional home, enhanced with such Southern-style touches as its welcoming covered porch with a metal roof and latticed supports. Yet its sturdy brick-and-siding exterior, ornamented by a single bay window, opens to a surprisingly expansive interior—its 3,000-plus square feet includes four bedrooms, three-and-a-half baths, and plenty of built-in features to help homeowners make the most of the space.

The living area begins with formal rooms—the foyer, living room, and dining room. The foyer provides space for art or fine furnishings. The living room, easily the home's largest room with nearly 400 square feet, is enhanced by a coffered ceiling as well as a fireplace

flanked by built-in bookcases. Take in the view of the rear property from the living room's the full-height windows or step outside to the covered porch. The dining room is an elegant setting for entertaining and works well with the kitchen, uniting the formal and informal spaces. Sleek stainless steel appliances and stunning tiled backsplashes combine with a convenient island snack bar that overlooks a keeping room with space for casual meals. The keeping room is also accessible from the wrap-around front porch —a feature that recognizes a family's tendency to enter the home from multiple points.

While the main living areas represent luxury and comfort, the rear portion of the plan is all about convenience. There

Above: Long sightlines through the center of the home encourage visitors to step farther inside.
Above Left: The wraparound porch adds a neighborly touch to the home, well-suited for a corner lot.
Left: The coffered ceiling and built-in shelves create an elegant, formal tone in the living room.

Above: Use the kitchen snack bar for eating
quick meals or keeping the family cook company.
Above Center & Above Right: Even a modest landscape
plan will enhance the home's seasonal living opportunities.
Right: The dining room is traditionally located at the front of the plan.

is a third entry to the home in the spacious two-car garage, near
the cozy home office. A mudroom provides a bench, built-in
shelves, and closet space for coats, boots, and backpacks, and a half
bath with extra space for linen storage adjoins the laundry area.

Bedrooms in this plan are as refined as the living spaces. In
the first-floor master suite, a bay window brings natural light
to the bedroom. Additional windows illuminate the bath,
which boasts a spa tub, corner walk-in shower, two vanities,
and a compartmented toilet. A walk-in closet features built-in
shelves. Walk-in closets are also included in two of the upstairs
bedrooms. Those two bedrooms share a bath; a third offers a
private bath. All three second-floor bedrooms share a study. ✿

POPLAR GROVE

PLAN #HPK3700074

Designed by Looney Ricks Kiss Architects, Inc.

First Floor: 2,133 sq. ft.

Second Floor: 983 sq. ft.

Total: 3,116 sq. ft.

Bedrooms: 4

Bathrooms: 3 ½

Width: 52' - 0"

Depth: 87' - 0"

Price Code: L4

Foundation: Slab

1-800-521-6797
eplans.com

First Floor

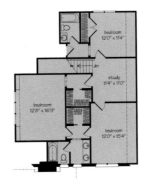

Second Floor

Inanda House

PLAN #HPK3700075

Designed by Mouzon Design
for Biltmore Estate

First Floor: 2,078 sq. ft.

Second Floor: 961 sq. ft.

Total: 3,039 sq. ft.

Width: 74' - 0"

Depth: 71' - 0"

Foundation: Crawlspace

Price Code: L4

1-800-850-1491
eplans.com

3 *Bedrooms* | **3** *Full Baths* | **1** *Half Bath*

BILTMORE™

For Your Home

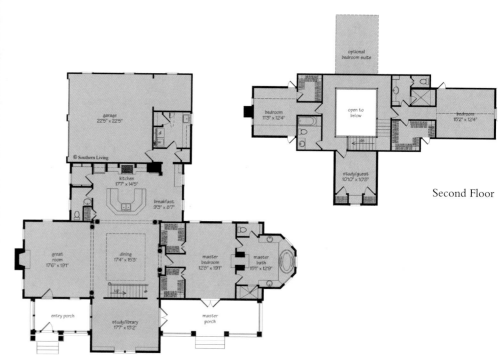

Second Floor

First Floor

Woodlawn

5 Bedrooms | 4 Full Baths

PLAN #HPK3700076

Designed by Bryan & Contreras, LLC

First Floor: 2,110 sq. ft.

Second Floor: 941 sq. ft.

Total: 3,051 sq. ft.

Width: 69' - 0"

Depth: 53' - 0"

Foundation: Unfinished Basement

Price Code: C3

1-800-850-1491
eplans.com

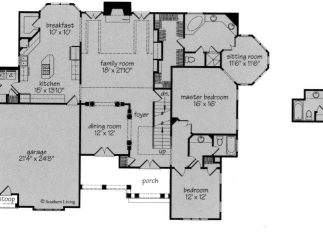

First Floor

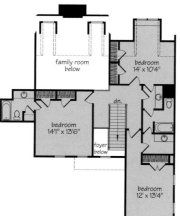

Second Floor

Clayfield Place

PLAN #HPK3700077

Designed by Looney Ricks Kiss
Architects, Inc.

First Floor: 2,252 sq. ft.

Second Floor: 818 sq. ft.

Total: 3,070 sq. ft.

Width: 99' - 0"

Depth: 44' - 0"

Foundation: Slab

Price Code: L1

1–800–850–1491
eplans.com

3 *Bedrooms* | 2 *Full Baths* | 1 *Half Bath*

© Southern Living

First Floor

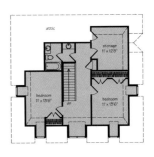

Second Floor

The Orchard House

3,084 square feet

| 4 *Bedrooms* | 4 *Full Baths* | 1 *Half Bath* |

PLAN #HPK3700078

Designed by Mouzon Design
for Biltmore Estate

First Floor: 2,240 sq. ft.

Second Floor: 844 sq. ft.

Total: 3,084 sq. ft.

Width: 77' – 0"

Depth: 74' – 6"

Foundation: Crawlspace

Price Code: L4

1–800–850–1491
eplans.com

First Floor

Second Floor

BILTMORE™
For Your Home

Brookwood Cottage

PLAN #HPK3700079

Designed by John Tee, Architect

First Floor: 2,272 sq. ft.

Second Floor: 828 sq. ft.

Total: 3,100 sq. ft.

Width: 65' - 0"

Depth: 60' - 0"

Foundation: Unfinished Basement

Price Code: L1

1–800–850–1491
eplans.com

3 Bedrooms | *4 Full Baths*

First Floor

Second Floor

Presque Isle

| 3 Bedrooms | 3 Full Baths | 1 Half Bath |

PLAN #HPK3700083

Designed by Gary/Ragsdale, Inc.

Square Footage: 3,113

Width: 69' – 0"

Depth: 79' – 0"

Foundation: Crawlspace

Price Code: C3

1–800–850–1491
eplans.com

OPTIONAL SUNROOM (253 sq. ft.)

Optional Layout

Myrtle Grove

PLAN #HPK3700081

Designed by Gary/Ragsdale, Inc.

Square Footage: 3,125

Width: 69' - 0"

Depth: 79' - 0"

Foundation: Crawlspace

Price Code: C3

1–800–850–1491
eplans.com

5 *Bedrooms* | 2 *Full Baths* | 1 *Half Bath*

Live Oak Cottage

3,153 square feet

3 *Bedrooms* | **3** *Full Baths* | **1** *Half Bath*

PLAN #HPK3700080

Designed by Looney Ricks Kiss Architects, Inc. for St. Joe Land Company

Square Footage: 3,153

Width: 80' - 0"

Depth: 91' - 0"

Foundation: Slab

Price Code: L4

1-800-850-1491
eplans.com

Scarborough

PLAN #HPK3700089

Designed by Gary/Ragsdale, Inc.

Square Footage: 3,154

Width: 70' – 0"

Depth: 80' – 0"

Foundation: Slab

Price Code: C3

1–800–850–1491
eplans.com

| 4 Bedrooms | 2 Full Baths | 1 Half Bath |

The Jefferson

5 *Bedrooms*	3 *Full Baths*	1 *Half Bath*

PLAN #HPK3700082

Designed by Gary/Ragsdale, Inc.

Square Footage: 3,165

Width: 69' - 0"

Depth: 79' - 0"

Foundation: Crawlspace

Price Code: C3

1–800–850–1491
eplans.com

master bedroom
15' x 21'

bedroom
14'8" x 11'

family room
18' x 22'

covered porch

optional room
12' x 19'4"

bedroom
11' x 13'

breakfast room
12'4" x 14'4"

kitchen
15' x 19'

covered porch

sunroom
12' x 19'4"

bedroom
11' x 13'

garage
21' x 21'

office/bedroom
11'6" x 16'6"

foyer

dining room
15' x 12'

porch

© Southern Living

Optional Layout

3,173 square feet

River Bluff

PLAN #HPK3700084

Designed by Mouzon Design

First Floor: 2,315 sq. ft.

Second Floor: 858 sq. ft.

Total: 3,173 sq. ft.

Width: 44' - 4"

Depth: 91' - 8"

Foundation: Crawlspace

Price Code: L2

1–800–850–1491
eplans.com

4 Bedrooms | *3 Full Baths* | *1 Half Bath*

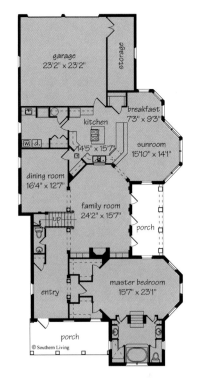

garage 23'2" x 23'2"

storage

breakfast 7'3" x 9'3"

kitchen 14'5" x 15'7"

sunroom 15'10" x 14'1"

w. d.

dining room 16'4" x 12'7"

family room 24'2" x 15'7"

porch

up

entry

master bedroom 15'7" x 23'1"

porch

© Southern Living

First Floor

open to below

dn.

bedroom 15'7" x 10'3"

bedroom 12'1" x 10'3"

porch

bedroom 11'2" x 10'11"

Second Floor

Lamberth Way

| 4 *Bedrooms* | 3 *Full Baths* | 1 *Half Bath* |

PLAN #HPK3700117

Designed by Sullivan Design Company

First Floor: 2,224 sq. ft.

Second Floor: 1,017 sq. ft.

Total: 3,241 sq. ft.

Width: 61' - 0"

Depth: 92' - 0"

Foundation: Crawlspace

Price Code: C3

1-800-850-1491
eplans.com

First Floor

Second Floor

3,180 square feet

2006 Cooking Light Fit House

PLAN #HPK3700085

Designed by John Tee, Architect
for Cooking Light Magazine

First Floor: 1,992 sq. ft.

Second Floor: 1,188 sq. ft.

Total: 3,180 sq. ft.

Width: 57' - 0"

Depth: 45' - 0"

Foundation: Unfinished Basement

Price Code: L2

1-800-850-1491
eplans.com

4 *Bedrooms* | 4 *Full Baths* | 1 *Half Bath*

First Floor

Second Floor

Bankston

| 4 *Bedrooms* | 3 *Full Baths* | 1 *Half Bath* |

PLAN #HPK3700164

Designed by Gary/Ragsdale, Inc.

Square Footage: 3,221

Width: 59' - 0"

Depth: 90' - 0"

Foundation: Slab

Price Code: C3

1-800-850-1491
eplans.com

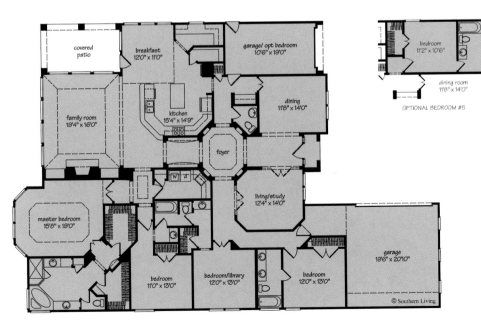

The Shoals

PLAN #HPK3700087

Designed by Mitchell Ginn

First Floor: 2,128 sq. ft.

Second Floor: 1,120 sq. ft.

Total: 3,248 sq. ft.

Width: 54' - 0"

Depth: 61' - 0"

Foundation: Unfinished Basement

Price Code: C3

1–800–850–1491
eplans.com

3 *Bedrooms* | 3 *Full Baths* | 1 *Half Bath*

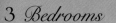

First Floor

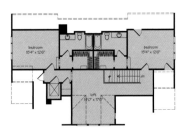

Second Floor

Optional Terrace

Shook Hill

4 *Bedrooms* | **3** *Full Baths* | **1** *Half Bath*

PLAN #HPK3700088

Designed by Mitchell Ginn

First Floor: 2,210 sq. ft.

Second Floor: 1,047 sq. ft.

Total: 3,257 sq. ft.

Width: 74' - 0"

Depth: 89' - 0"

Foundation: Unfinished Basement

Price Code: L1

1–800–850–1491
eplans.com

garage
33'4" x 21'4"

© Southern Living

porch

porch

breakfast room
10'4" x 15'2"

master bedroom
16'2" x 15'4"

family room
18" x 19'10"

kitchen
11'8" x 17'6"

up   dn.

w.d.

dining room
12' x 15'4"

study
14'8" x 12'4"

foyer

porch

First Floor

bedroom
15'4" x 13'4"

bedroom
16'4" x 11'8"

dn.

bedroom
12' x 14'2"

Second Floor

3,273 square feet

Howell Park

PLAN #HPK3700090

Designed by Mitchell Ginn

First Floor: 2,303 sq. ft.

Second Floor: 970 sq. ft.

Total: 3,273 sq. ft.

Width: 62' - 0"

Depth: 62' - 0"

Foundation: Basement/Slab

Price Code: L1

1–800–850–1491
eplans.com

4 *Bedrooms* | 3 *Full Baths* | 1 *Half Bath*

First Floor

Second Floor

New Willow Grove

3,316 square feet

| 4 *Bedrooms* | 4 *Full Baths* | 1 *Half Bath* |

PLAN #HPK3700091

Designed by John Tee, Architect

First Floor: 2,368 sq. ft.

Second Floor: 948 sq. ft.

Total: 3,316 sq. ft.

Width: 71' - 0"

Depth: 57' - 0"

Foundation: Crawlspace

Price Code: L1

1–800–850–1491
eplans.com

First Floor

Second Floor

Crescent Hill

PLAN #HPK3700092

Designed by Gary/Ragsdale, Inc.

First Floor: 2,450 sq. ft.

Second Floor: 885 sq. ft.

Total: 3,335 sq. ft.

Width: 66' - 0"

Depth: 75' - 0"

Foundation: Crawlspace

Price Code: C3

1–800–850–1491
eplans.com

4 *Bedrooms* | 3 *Full Baths* | 1 *Half Bath*

First Floor

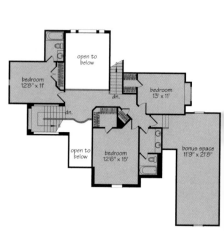

Second Floor

Biddleford

4 *Bedrooms* | 3 *Full Baths* | 1 *Half Bath*

PLAN #HPK3700093

Designed by Gary/Ragsdale, Inc.

First Floor: 2,450 sq. ft.

Second Floor: 885 sq. ft.

Total: 3,335 sq. ft.

Width: 66' – 0"

Depth: 75' – 0"

Foundation: Crawlspace

Price Code: C3

1–800–850–1491
eplans.com

First Floor

Second Floor

Van Buren

PLAN #HPK3700094

Designed by Gary/Ragsdale, Inc.

First Floor: 2,450 sq. ft.

Second Floor: 885 sq. ft.

Total: 3,335 sq. ft.

Width: 66' - 0"

Depth: 75' - 0"

Foundation: Crawlspace

Price Code: C3

1–800–850–1491
eplans.com

4 Bedrooms | *3 Full Baths* | *1 Half Bath*

First Floor

Second Floor

Monet House

| 4 *Bedrooms* | 4 *Full Baths* |

PLAN #HPK3700095

Designed by Bryan & Contreras, LLC

First Floor: 1,732 sq. ft.

Second Floor: 1,643 sq. ft.

Total: 3,375 sq. ft.

Width: 52' – 0"

Depth: 42' – 0"

Foundation: Slab

Price Code: C3

1–800–850–1491
eplans.com

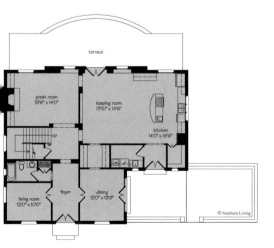

First Floor

Second Floor

Denham Springs

PLAN #HPK3700097

Designed by John Tee, Architect

First Floor: 2,414 sq. ft.

Second Floor: 998 sq. ft.

Total: 3,412 sq. ft.

Width: 71' - 0"

Depth: 57' - 0"

Foundation: Crawlspace

Price Code: L2

1–800–850–1491
eplans.com

5 *Bedrooms* | **4** *Full Baths* | **1** *Half Bath*

First Floor

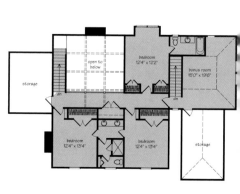

Second Floor

Clenney Point

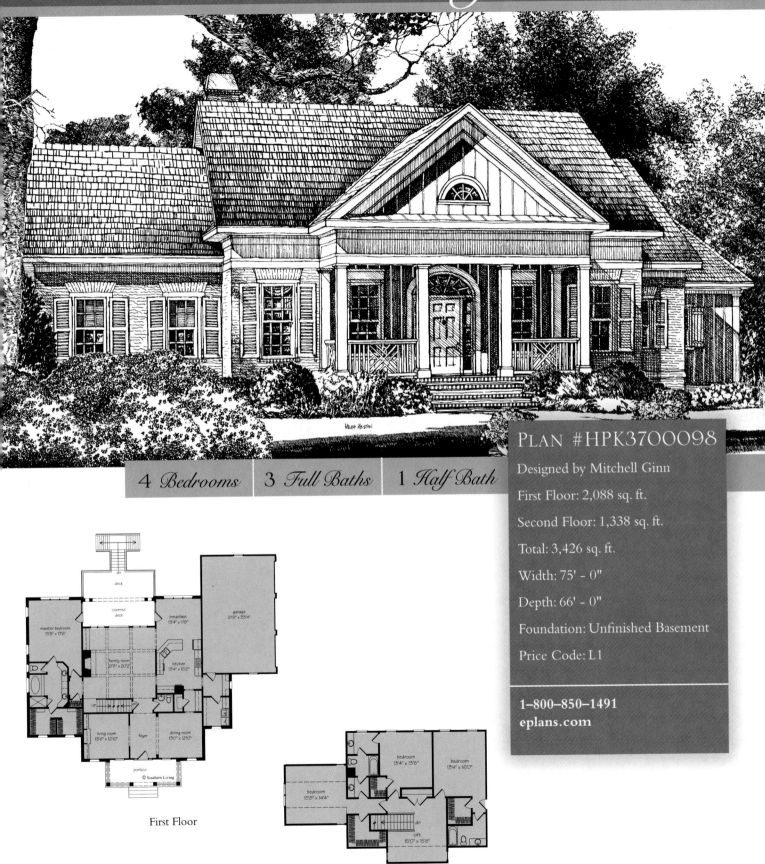

4 *Bedrooms* | **3** *Full Baths* | **1** *Half Bath*

PLAN #HPK3700098

Designed by Mitchell Ginn

First Floor: 2,088 sq. ft.

Second Floor: 1,338 sq. ft.

Total: 3,426 sq. ft.

Width: 75' - 0"

Depth: 66' - 0"

Foundation: Unfinished Basement

Price Code: L1

1-800-850-1491
eplans.com

First Floor

Second Floor

Lexington

PLAN #HPK3700099

Designed by Gary/Ragsdale, Inc.

First Floor: 2,626 sq. ft.

Second Floor: 803 sq. ft.

Total: 3,429 sq. ft.

Width: 55' - 0"

Depth: 102' - 0"

Foundation: Slab

Price Code: C3

1–800–850–1491
eplans.com

4 *Bedrooms* | 3 *Full Baths*

First Floor

Second Floor

Aaronwood

| 3 *Bedrooms* | 3 *Full Baths* | 1 *Half Bath* |

PLAN #HPK3700100

Designed by Bryan & Contreras, LLC

First Floor: 2,612 sq. ft.

Second Floor: 840 sq. ft.

Total: 3,452 sq. ft.

Width: 83' – 0"

Depth: 115' – 0"

Foundation: Unfinished Basement

Price Code: L1

1–800–850–1491
eplans.com

First Floor

Second Floor

Brookfield

PLAN #HPK3700101

Designed by Caldwell–Cline
Architects & Designers, Inc.

First Floor: 2,645 sq. ft.

Second Floor: 852 sq. ft.

Total: 3,497 sq. ft.

Width: 95' - 0"

Depth: 60' - 0"

Foundation: Crawlspace,
Unfinished Basement

Price Code: L4

1–800–850–1491
eplans.com

3 Bedrooms | *4 Full Baths*

First Floor

Second Floor

Optional Terrace

STONES RIVER

Rural Revisited

An ambitious design blends the
traditional and the contemporary

Sleek, modernist lines

guide the exterior of this Craftsman-inspired cottage. Designed for 360-degree views every side features tall windows and architectural points of interest. Seasonal interior rooms and 1,200 square feet of porch space offer a soothing alternative to air conditioning and heating—the country breeze. For example, the second-floor media room opens to a nearly 300-square-foot sleeping porch.

Exterior elements of the home are simply crafted, although decorative detailing has been added to the roof eaves. Lap siding with a narrow 5-inch overlap and shingles finish the home. Timber posts and brick piers support the roof and porch deck.

Historically, rural homes were built for expansion. The initial construction would be followed, in flush

Left: Each of the second floor bedrooms receives unique views of the property.

Below: A decorative ceiling helps define the kitchen, which opens onto the breakfast nook and family room.

Opposite: A hanging bed is a perfect rustic detail for this home.

Previous Page: Designed for panoramic views, the home is perfect for rural landscapes. The distinctive metal roof offers unparalleled durability and adds a contemporizing touch to the home's traditional architecture.

STONES RIVER

PLAN #HPK3700102

Designed by Looney Ricks
Kiss Architects, Inc. for
The Progressive Farmer

First Floor: 2,548 sq. ft.

Second Floor: 1,368 sq. ft.

Total: 3,916 sq. ft.

Bedrooms: 4

Bathrooms: 5

Width: 97' - 0"

Depth: 87' - 0"

Foundation: Crawlspace

Price Code: L4

1–800–521–6797
eplans.com

First Floor

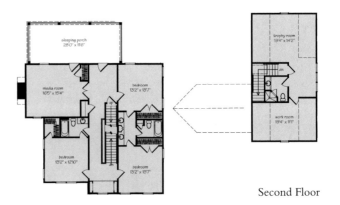

Second Floor

ears, by additions that housed new needs for a growing mily. Stones River recreates that building style. The entral portion of the house features a main living area its center, comprising the kitchen, breakfast area, and mily room. Beams and three pairs of French doors ad from this area to a large, screened outdoor room. n mild weather, this porch increases the usable space of ie kitchen and family room. One wing of the home—a ructure harkening back to the tradition of adding onto ie house—holds the master suite.

The house showcases a mudroom, laundry room, and ome office, all located together for efficiency. This part f the floor plan recognizes that the side entrance will e the most frequently used point of entry for the family id provides organizing spaces for members to off-load ersonal items upon entry. A special mudroom feature is ie canine care center, which includes dog-food storage,

a fresh water tap, and a shower outfitted for both human and pet use.

The 200-square-foot kitchen is the home's hub, with an open view of the family room. The kitchen and dining room are connected by a true butler's pantry. Opposite the dining room is versatile space for a library or formal living room.

Rather than ceremonial stairs in the foyer, a second, kitchen stairway is located for utility.

Upstairs are three bedrooms; a pair connected by a common bathroom. A fourth room, the media room, opens to guests through double doors. Designed to view movies, play video games, or enjoy music, this room will be wired for cutting-edge video and audio technology. ❋

Kinsley Place

PLAN #HPK3700103

Designed by Looney Ricks Kiss Architects, Inc. for St. Joe Land Company

First Floor: 2,692 sq. ft.

Second Floor: 818 sq. ft.

Total: 3,510 sq. ft.

Width: 64' - 0"

Depth: 122' - 0"

Foundation: Slab

Price Code: SQ3

1–800–850–1491
eplans.com

4 *Bedrooms* | 5 *Full Baths* | 1 *Half Bath*

First Floor

Second Floor

4 *Bedrooms* | 4 *Full Baths*

First Floor

Second Floor

PLAN #HPK3700104

Designed by Mouzon Design for Biltmore Estate

First Floor: 2,410 sq. ft.

Second Floor: 1,100 sq. ft.

Total: 3,510 sq. ft.

Width: 71' - 0"

Depth: 79' - 0"

Foundation: Crawlspace

Price Code: L4

1-800-850-1491
eplans.com

BILTMORE™
For Your Home

Danbury Oaks

PLAN #HPK3700106

Designed by Gary/Ragsdale, Inc.

First Floor: 2,712 sq. ft.

Second Floor: 826 sq. ft.

Total: 3,538 sq. ft.

Width: 55' - 0"

Depth: 101' - 0"

Foundation: Slab

Price Code: L1

1-800-850-1491
eplans.com

3 *Bedrooms* | 3 *Full Baths* | 1 *Half Bath*

First Floor

Second Floor

Crestview Park

| 4 *Bedrooms* | 4 *Full Baths* | 1 *Half Bath* |

PLAN #HPK3700107

Designed by Gary/Ragsdale, Inc.

First Floor: 2,053 sq. ft.

Second Floor: 1,531 sq. ft.

Total: 3,584 sq. ft.

Width: 69' – 0"

Depth: 54' – 0"

Foundation: Slab

Price Code: L1

1–800–850–1491
eplans.com

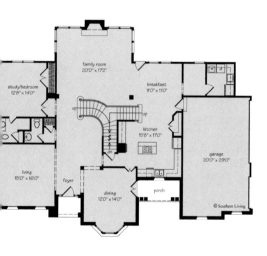

First Floor

Second Floor

Abberley Lane

PLAN #HPK3700108

Designed by John Tee, Architect

First Floor: 2,686 sq. ft.

Second Floor: 1,130 sq. ft.

Total: 3,816 sq. ft.

Width: 78' - 0"

Depth: 62' - 0"

Foundation: Crawlspace

Price Code: L4

1–800–850–1491
eplans.com

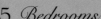

5 *Bedrooms* | 4 *Full Baths* | 1 *Half Bath*

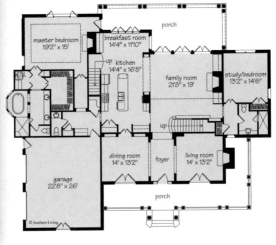

First Floor

Second Floor

Rucker Place

| 5 *Bedrooms* | 4 *Full Baths* | 1 *Half Bath* |

PLAN #HPK3700109

Designed by Looney Ricks Kiss Architects, Inc.

First Floor: 2,351 sq. ft.

Second Floor: 1,273 sq. ft.

Total: 3,624 sq. ft.

Width: 83' - 0"

Depth: 54' - 0"

Foundation: Crawlspace, Pier (same as Piling)

Price Code: L1

1–800–850–1491
eplans.com

First Floor

Second Floor

Newberry Park

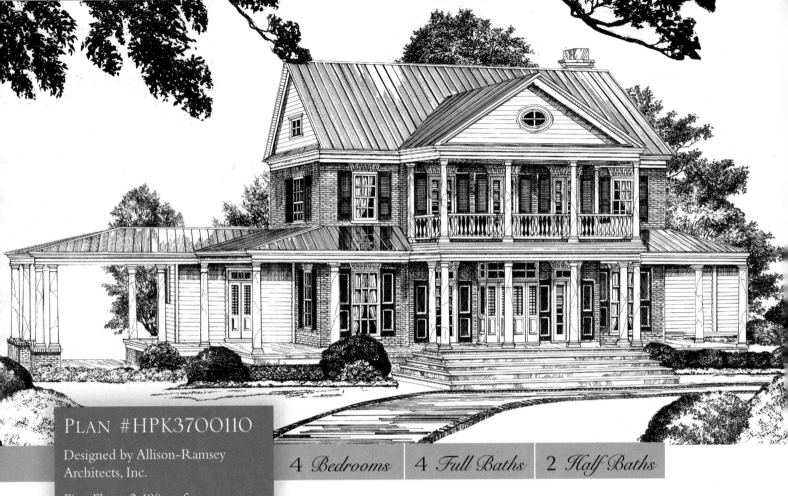

PLAN #HPK3700110

Designed by Allison-Ramsey Architects, Inc.

First Floor: 2,490 sq. ft.

Second Floor: 1,135 sq. ft.

Total: 3,625 sq. ft.

Width: 87' - 0"

Depth: 62' - 0"

Foundation: Crawlspace

Price Code: L4

1-800-850-1491
eplans.com

4 *Bedrooms* | 4 *Full Baths* | 2 *Half Baths*

First Floor

Second Floor

Avington Place

| 4 Bedrooms | 3 Full Baths | 2 Half Baths |

PLAN #HPK3700111

Designed by John Tee, Architect

First Floor: 2,516 sq. ft.

Second Floor: 1,113 sq. ft.

Total: 3,629 sq. ft.

Width: 80' - 0"

Depth: 59' - 0"

Foundation: Crawlspace

Price Code: L1

1–800–850–1491
eplans.com

First Floor

Second Floor

Cypress Garden

PLAN #HPK3700112

Designed by Looney Ricks Kiss Architects, Inc.

First Floor: 2,507 sq. ft.

Second Floor: 1,134 sq. ft.

Total: 3,641 sq. ft.

Width: 70' - 0"

Depth: 55' - 0"

Foundation: Crawlspace

Price Code: L1

1–800–850–1491
eplans.com

| 4 *Bedrooms* | 4 *Full Baths* | 1 *Half Bath* |

First Floor

Second Floor

4 *Bedrooms* | **3** *Full Baths* | **1** *Half Bath*

PLAN #HPK3700152

Designed by Mitchell Ginn

First Floor: 2,113 sq. ft.

Second Floor: 1,538 sq. ft.

Total: 3,651 sq. ft.

Width: 54' – 0"

Depth: 62' – 0"

Foundation: Unfinished Basement

Price Code: L1

1–800–850–1491
eplans.com

Optional Basement

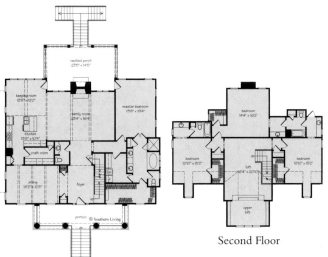

First Floor

Second Floor

3,655 square feet

Smythe Park House

PLAN #HPK3700113

Designed by Mitchell Ginn

First Floor: 1,884 sq. ft.

Second Floor: 1,627 sq. ft.

Total: 3,655 sq. ft.

Width: 60' – 0"

Depth: 105' – 0"

Foundation: Crawlspace

Price Code: L4

1–800–850–1491

eplans.com

4 *Bedrooms* | 4 *Full Baths* | 1 *Half Bath*

First Floor

Second Floor

Amelia Place

5 *Bedrooms* | **4** *Full Baths*

PLAN #HPK3700115

Designed by John Tee, Architect

First Floor: 2,617 sq. ft.

Second Floor: 1,042 sq. ft.

Total: 3,659 sq. ft.

Width: 79' - 0"

Depth: 66' - 0"

Foundation: Crawlspace

Price Code: L4

1–800–850–1491
eplans.com

First Floor

Second Floor

Belfield Bend

PLAN #HPK3700114

Designed by John Tee, Architect

First Floor: 2,321 sq. ft.

Second Floor: 1,339 sq. ft.

Total: 3,660 sq. ft.

Width: 78' – 0"

Depth: 52' – 0"

Foundation: Crawlspace

Price Code: L2

1–800–850–1491
eplans.com

5 *Bedrooms*   5 *Full Baths*   2 *Half Baths*

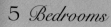

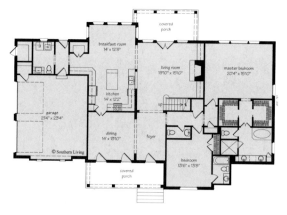

First Floor

Second Floor

Chatham Hall

3,666 square feet

| 4 *Bedrooms* | 3 *Full Baths* | 2 *Half Baths* |

PLAN #HPK3700116

Designed by Bryan & Contreras, LLC

First Floor: 2,669 sq. ft.

Second Floor: 997 sq. ft.

Total: 3,666 sq. ft.

Width: 105' - 0"

Depth: 51' - 0"

Foundation: Unfinished Basement

Price Code: L2

1-800-850-1491
eplans.com

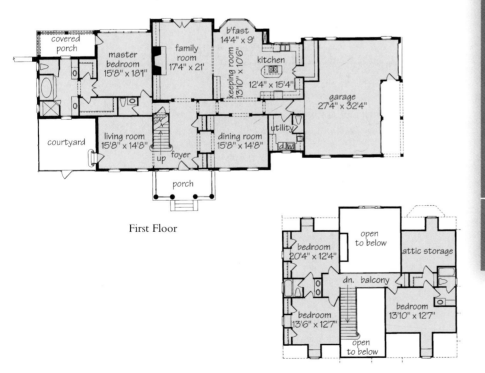

First Floor

Second Floor

Brenthaven

PLAN #HPK3700151

Designed by Looney Ricks Kiss Architects, Inc.

First Floor: 3,011 sq. ft.

Second Floor: 663 sq. ft.

Total: 3,674 sq. ft.

Width: 111' - 0"

Depth: 83' - 0"

Foundation: Slab, Unfinished Basement

Price Code: L4

1–800–850–1491
eplans.com

3 *Bedrooms* | 4 *Full Baths* | 1 *Half Bath*

First Floor

Second Floor

Belvedere

5 *Bedrooms* | 5 *Full Baths*

PLAN #HPK3700105

Designed by Looney Ricks Kiss Architects, Inc.

First Floor: 2,285 sq. ft.

Second Floor: 1,402 sq. ft.

Total: 3,687 sq. ft.

Width: 56' - 0"

Depth: 85' - 0"

Foundation: Slab

Price Code: L1

1-800-850-1491
eplans.com

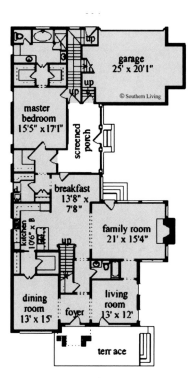

First Floor

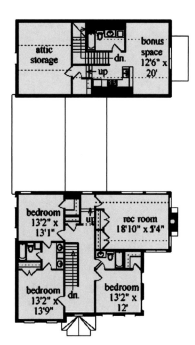

Second Floor

PLAN #HPK3700118

Designed by Mouzon Design

First Floor: 2,746 sq. ft.

Second Floor: 944 sq. ft.

Total: 3,690 sq. ft.

Width: 71' - 0"

Depth: 100' - 0"

Foundation: Crawlspace

Price Code: L2

1–800–850–1491
eplans.com

3 Bedrooms | *3 Full Baths* | *1 Half Bath*

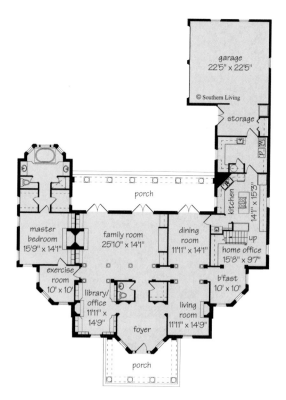

First Floor

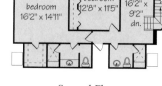

Second Floor

Ansley Park

4 *Bedrooms*	3 *Full Baths*	1 *Half Bath*

PLAN #HPK3700119

Designed by Bryan & Contreras, LLC

First Floor: 2,602 sq. ft.

Second Floor: 1,087 sq. ft.

Total: 3,690 sq. ft.

Width: 97' - 0"

Depth: 64' - 0"

Foundation: Unfinished Basement

Price Code: L1

1–800–850–1491
eplans.com

First Floor

Second Floor

PLAN #HPK3700120

Designed by Mouzon Design for Biltmore Estate

First Floor: 2,376 sq. ft.

Second Floor: 1,327 sq. ft.

Total: 3,703 sq. ft.

Width: 98' - 0"

Depth: 63' - 0"

Foundation: Crawlspace

Price Code: L4

1-800-850-1491
eplans.com

| 4 *Bedrooms* | 3 *Full Baths* | 1 *Half Bath* |

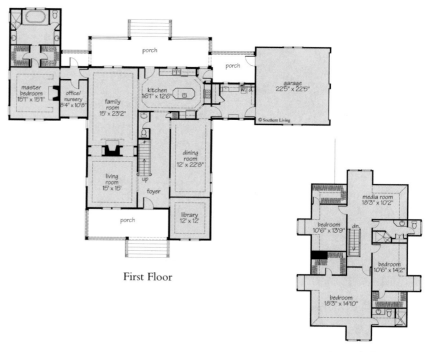

First Floor

Second Floor

BILTMORE™

For Your Home

Weston House

4 *Bedrooms* | **4** *Full Baths*

First Floor

Second Floor

PLAN #HPK37OO121

Designed by Mouzon Design for Biltmore Estate

First Floor: 2,629 sq. ft.

Second Floor: 1,077 sq. ft.

Total: 3,706 sq. ft.

Width: 65' - 0"

Depth: 91' - 0"

Foundation: Crawlspace

Price Code: L4

1–800–850–1491
eplans.com

BILTMORE™
For Your Home

3,757 square feet

Crabapple Cottage

PLAN #HPK3700131

Designed by John Tee, Architect

First Floor: 2,674 sq. ft.

Second Floor: 1,083 sq. ft.

Total: 3,757 sq. ft.

Width: 76' - 0"

Depth: 90' - 0"

Foundation: Unfinished Basement

Price Code: L4

1–800–850–1491
eplans.com

4 Bedrooms | *3 Full Baths* | *2 Half Baths*

porch

master bedroom 14'1" x 19'9"

living room 22' x 15'8"

family room 16' x 25'

dining room 13' x 14'8"

kitchen 14' x 14'

up

foyer

front porch

office 10' x 14'

deck

garage 24' x 22'

© Southern Living

First Floor

bedroom 14' x 12'

open to below

bedroom 14'3" x 14'

bedroom 14' x 12'

loft 13'6" x 14'

dn

storage

dn

bonus room 15' x 22'

Second Floor

Sterett Springs

| 4 *Bedrooms* | 4 *Full Baths* | 1 *Half Bath* |

PLAN #HPK3700056

Designed by John Tee, Architect

First Floor: 2,674 sq. ft.

Second Floor: 3,758 sq. ft.

Total: 2,782 sq. ft.

Width: 77' - 0"

Depth: 73' - 0"

Foundation: Crawlspace

Price Code: L1

1–800–850–1491
eplans.com

First Floor

Second Floor

Brittingham

PLAN #HPK3700122

Designed by Mitchell Ginn

First Floor: 2,462 sq. ft.

Second Floor: 1,308 sq. ft.

Total: 3,770 sq. ft.

Width: 68' - 0"

Depth: 57' - 0"

Foundation: Unfinished Basement

Price Code: L1

1–800–850–1491

eplans.com

5 *Bedrooms* | 4 *Full Baths*

First Floor

Second Floor

Greywell Cottage

4 *Bedrooms*	3 *Full Baths*	2 *Half Baths*

PLAN #HPK3700123

Designed by Frusterio & Associates

First Floor: 2,051 sq. ft.

Second Floor: 1,517 sq. ft.

Total: 3,781 sq. ft.

Width: 66' – 0"

Depth: 48' – 0"

Foundation: Unfinished Basement

Price Code: L4

1–800–850–1491
eplans.com

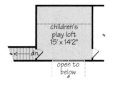

First Floor

Second Floor

Rockwell House

PLAN #HPK3700124

Designed by Mitchell Ginn

First Floor: 2,347 sq. ft.

Second Floor: 1,436 sq. ft.

Total: 3,783 sq. ft.

Width: 72' - 0"

Depth: 82' - 0"

Foundation: Unfinished Basement

Price Code: L1

1-800-850-1491
eplans.com

4 *Bedrooms* | 3 *Full Baths* | 1 *Half Bath*

First Floor

Second Floor

Braden House

| 3 *Bedrooms* | 4 *Full Baths* | 1 *Half Bath* |

PLAN #HPK3700125

Designed by Caldwell-Cline
Architects & Designers
for Cooking Light Magazine

First Floor: 2,366 sq. ft.

Second Floor: 1,436 sq. ft.

Total: 3,802 sq. ft.

Width: 86' - 0"

Depth: 63' - 0"

Foundation: Unfinished Basement

Price Code: L4

1–800–850–1491
eplans.com

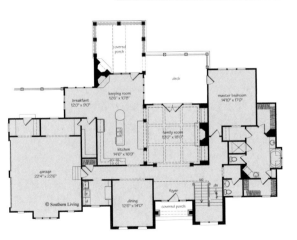

First Floor

Second Floor

Sagewick House

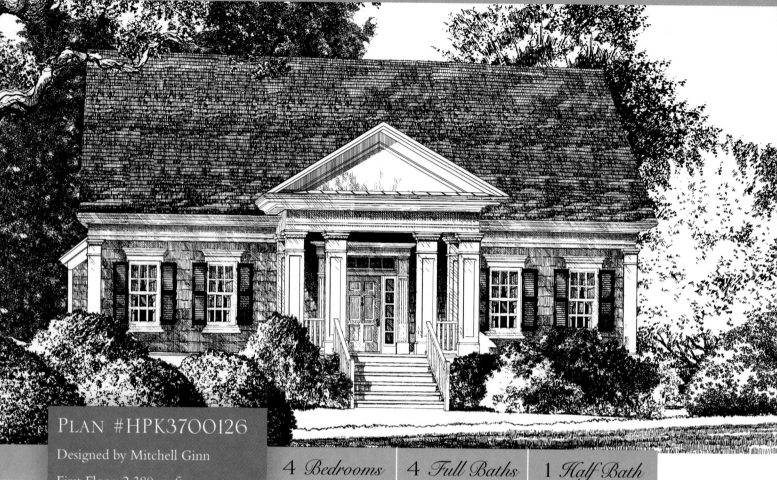

PLAN #HPK3700126

Designed by Mitchell Ginn

First Floor: 2,380 sq. ft.

Second Floor: 1,430 sq. ft.

Total: 3,810 sq. ft.

Width: 65' - 0"

Depth: 27' - 0"

Foundation: Unfinished Basement

Price Code: L1

1–800–850–1491
eplans.com

4 *Bedrooms* | 4 *Full Baths* | 1 *Half Bath*

Second Floor

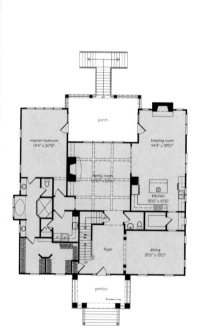

First Floor

Claremont

| 4 *Bedrooms* | 3 *Full Baths* | 1 *Half Bath* |

PLAN #HPK3700127

Designed by Gary/Ragsdale, Inc.

First Floor: 2,485 sq. ft.

Second Floor: 1,327 sq. ft.

Total: 3,812 sq. ft.

Width: 74' - 0"

Depth: 58' - 0"

Foundation: Slab

Price Code: L1

1–800–850–1491
eplans.com

First Floor

Second Floor

Whitfield II

PLAN #HPK3700128

Designed by Bryan & Contreras, LLC

First Floor: 3,000 sq. ft.

Second Floor: 854 sq. ft.

Total: 3,854 sq. ft.

Width: 110' - 0"

Depth: 67' - 0"

Foundation: Unfinished Basement

Price Code: L1

1–800–850–1491
eplans.com

3 *Bedrooms* | 3 *Full Baths* | 1 *Half Bath*

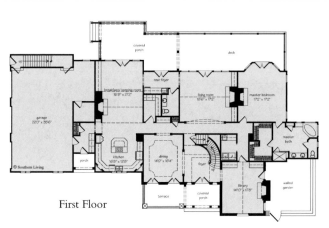

First Floor

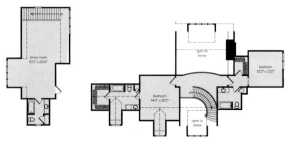

Second Floor

Mulberry Park

| 4 *Bedrooms* | 4 *Full Baths* | 1 *Half Bath* |

PLAN #HPK3700096

Designed by Looney Ricks Kiss Architects, Inc.

First Floor: 2,013 sq. ft.

Second Floor: 1,826 sq. ft.

Total: 3,899 sq. ft.

Width: 57' - 5"

Depth: 85' - 2"

Foundation: Slab

Price Code: L4

1-800-850-1491
eplans.com

garden

office/studio
15'2" x 20'8"

pergola

garage
20'7" x 25'10"

potting room

© Southern Living

garden courtyard

up

porch

family room
15' x 20'

office
8'9" x 7'4"

side entry

sunroom
15'4" x 14'3"

b'fast
10'6" x 14'

kitchen
10' x 18

butler's pantry

study/
guestroom
14'2" x 12'1"

foyer/dining hall
14'2" x 22'

portico

First Floor

guest apartment
17'7" x 17'4"

dn.

balcony

master bedroom
16'9" x 16'10"

morning bar

dn.

up

nursery
12'4" x 13'5"

comp. nook
7'6" x 10'1"

boy's bedroom
11'8" x 14'2"

Second Floor

Sabine River Cottage

PLAN #HPK3700130

Designed by John Tee, Architect

First Floor: 2,722 sq. ft.

Second Floor: 1,218 sq. ft.

Total: 3,940 sq. ft.

Width: 74' – 6"

Depth: 85' – 4"

Foundation: Unfinished Basement

Price Code: L2

1–800–850–1491
eplans.com

4 *Bedrooms* | 3 *Full Baths* | 2 *Half Baths*

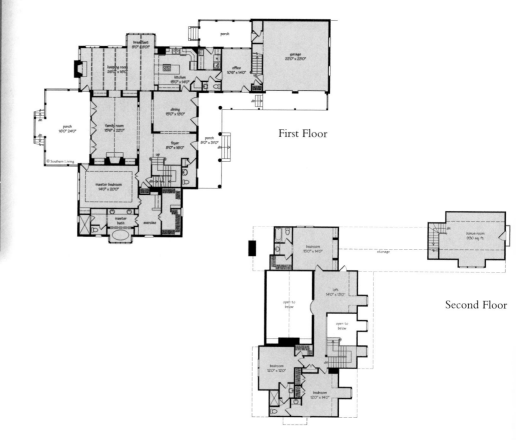

First Floor

Second Floor

Colonial Lake Cottage

5 *Bedrooms* | 4 *Full Baths*

PLAN #HPK3700132

Designed by Looney Ricks Kiss Architects, Inc.

First Floor: 2,304 sq. ft.

Second Floor: 1,725 sq. ft.

Total: 4,029 sq. ft.

Width: 57' - 0"

Depth: 117' - 0"

Foundation: Slab

Price Code: L1

1-800-850-1491
eplans.com

First Floor

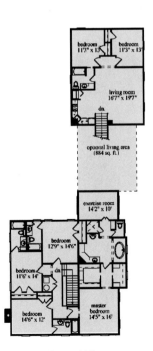

Second Floor

Walker's Bluff

PLAN #HPK3700133

Designed by Gary/Ragsdale, Inc.

First Floor: 2,570 sq. ft.

Second Floor: 1,465 sq. ft.

Total: 4,035 sq. ft.

Width: 61' - 0"

Depth: 76' - 0"

Foundation: Slab

Price Code: L4

1–800–850–1491
eplans.com

4 *Bedrooms* | 4 *Full Baths* | 1 *Half Bath*

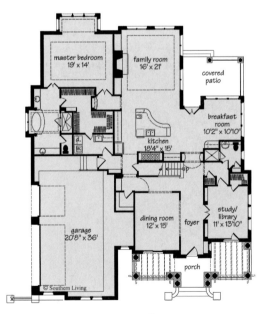

First Floor

Second Floor

Pine Glen

| 3 Bedrooms | 3 Full Baths | 2 Half Baths |

First Floor

© Southern Living

Second Floor

PLAN #HPK3700134

Designed by Looney Ricks Kiss Architects, Inc.

First Floor: 2,921 sq. ft.

Second Floor: 1,116 sq. ft.

Total: 4,037 sq. ft.

Width: 98' – 0"

Depth: 103' – 0"

Foundation: Crawlspace

Price Code: L2

1–800–850–1491
eplans.com

Sienna Park

PLAN #HPK3700135

Designed by RPGA Design Group, Inc.

First Floor: 2,849 sq. ft.

Second Floor: 1,198 sq. ft.

Total: 4,047 sq. ft.

Width: 94' - 0"

Depth: 58' - 0"

Foundation: Slab

Price Code: L2

1–800–850–1491
eplans.com

| 4 *Bedrooms* | 4 *Full Baths* | 1 *Half Bath* |

First Floor

Second Floor

Forest Glen

| 4 *Bedrooms* | 3 *Full Baths* | 1 *Half Bath* |

PLAN #HPK3700136

Designed by Gary/Ragsdale, Inc.

First Floor: 2,649 sq. ft.

Second Floor: 1,410 sq. ft.

Total: 4,059 sq. ft.

Width: 83' - 0"

Depth: 59' - 0"

Foundation: Slab

Price Code: C4

1-800-850-1491
eplans.com

First Floor

Second Floor

Luberon

PLAN #HPK3700129

Designed by Gary/Ragsdale, Inc.

First Floor: 2,518 sq. ft.

Second Floor: 1,582 sq. ft.

Total: 4,100 sq. ft.

Width: 62' - 0"

Depth: 74' - 0"

Foundation: Slab

Price Code: L1

1-800-850-1491

eplans.com

5 *Bedrooms* | 4 *Full Baths*

First Floor

Second Floor

Travis Ridge

| 3 Bedrooms | 3 Full Baths |

PLAN #HPK3700165

Designed by George Graves, AIA

First Floor: 3,296 sq. ft.

Second Floor: 805 sq. ft.

Total: 4,101 sq. ft.

Width: 85' – 0"

Depth: 111' – 0"

Foundation: Slab

Price Code: L4

1–800–850–1491
eplans.com

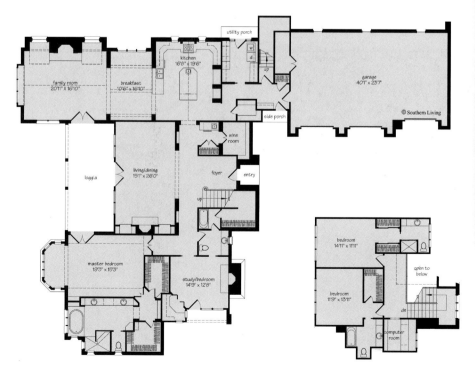

First Floor

Second Floor

Riddley Park

PLAN #HPK3700138

Designed by Looney Ricks Kiss Architects, Inc.

First Floor: 2,767 sq. ft.

Second Floor: 1,370 sq. ft.

Total: 4,137 sq. ft.

Width: 74' - 0"

Depth: 97' - 0"

Foundation: Crawlspace

Price Code: L2

1-800-850-1491
eplans.com

4 *Bedrooms* | 3 *Full Baths* | 1 *Half Bath*

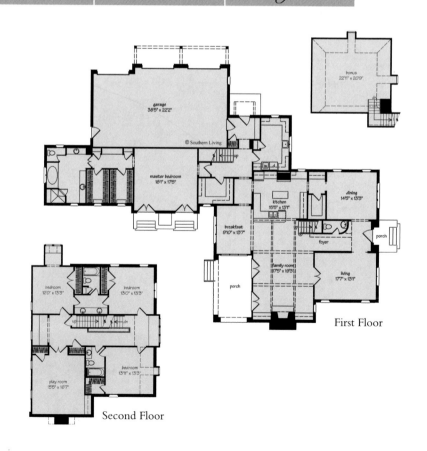

First Floor

Second Floor

| 4 *Bedrooms* | 4 *Full Baths* | 1 *Half Bath* |

PLAN #HPK3700139

Designed by Bryan & Contreras, LLC

First Floor: 3,166 sq. ft.

Second Floor: 992 sq. ft.

Total: 4,158 sq. ft.

Width: 107' - 0"

Depth: 76' - 0"

Foundation: Unfinished Basement

Price Code: L1

1-800-850-1491
eplans.com

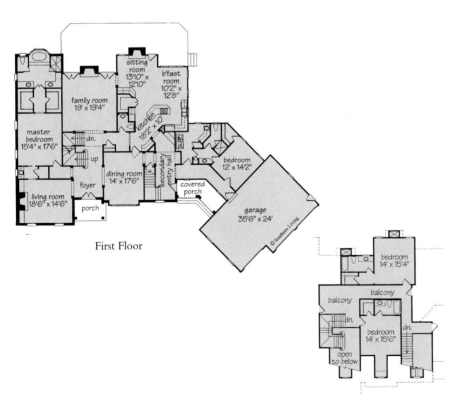

First Floor

- sitting room 13'10" x 12'10"
- b'fast room 10'2" x 12'8"
- family room 19' x 19'4"
- kitchen 18'2" x 10'
- master bedroom 15'4" x 17'6"
- dn.
- up
- dining room 14' x 17'6"
- Secondary entry hall
- bedroom 12' x 14'2"
- foyer
- covered porch
- living room 18'6" x 14'6"
- porch
- garage 35'6" x 24'

© Southern Living

Second Floor

- bedroom 14' x 15'4"
- balcony
- balcony
- dn.
- bedroom 14' x 15'6"
- dn.
- open to below

Harwood Park

PLAN #HPK3700140

Designed by Cornerstone Group
Architects

First Floor: 2,861 sq. ft.

Second Floor: 1,310 sq. ft.

Total: 4,171 sq. ft.

Width: 102' - 0"

Depth: 81' - 0"

Foundation: Slab

Price Code: L1

1-800-850-1491
eplans.com

| 4 *Bedrooms* | 3 *Full Baths* | 1 *Half Bath* |

First Floor

Second Floor

Wilmington Place

| 4 Bedrooms | 4 Full Baths | 1 Half Bath |

PLAN #HPK3700141

Designed by Gary/Ragsdale, Inc.

First Floor: 2,866 sq. ft.

Second Floor: 1,320 sq. ft.

Total: 4,186 sq. ft.

Width: 62' - 0"

Depth: 100' - 0"

Foundation: Slab

Price Code: L1

1–800–850–1491
eplans.com

First Floor

Second Floor

Stanton Court

PLAN #HPK3700142

Designed by Bryan & Contreras, LLC

First Floor: 3,000 sq. ft.

Second Floor: 1,206 sq. ft.

Total: 4,206 sq. ft.

Width: 110' - 0"

Depth: 67' - 0"

Foundation: Unfinished Basement

Price Code: L1

1–800–850–1491
eplans.com

| 4 Bedrooms | 4 Full Baths | 1 Half Bath |

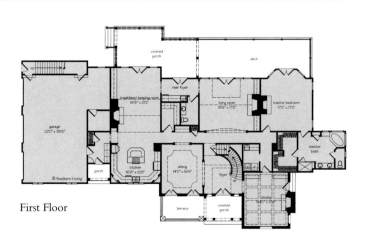

First Floor

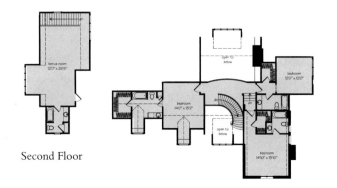

Second Floor

Cambridge

5 *Bedrooms* | 4 *Full Baths* | 1 *Half Bath*

PLAN #HPK3700143

Designed by Gary/Ragsdale, Inc.

First Floor: 2,597 sq. ft.

Second Floor: 1,631 sq. ft.

Total: 4,228 sq. ft.

Width: 60' - 0"

Depth: 86' - 0"

Foundation: Slab

Price Code: L1

1–800–850–1491
eplans.com

First Floor

Second Floor

Strathmore

PLAN #HPK3700144

Designed by Gary/Ragsdale, Inc.

First Floor: 2,901 sq. ft.

Second Floor: 1,389 sq. ft.

Total: 4,290 sq. ft.

Width: 73' - 0"

Depth: 80' - 0"

Foundation: Slab

Price Code: L1

1–800–850–1491
eplans.com

4 *Bedrooms* | 4 *Full Baths* | 1 *Half Bath*

First Floor

Second Floor

Whitfield

5 *Bedrooms* | **4** *Full Baths* | **1** *Half Bath*

PLAN #HPK3700145

Designed by Bryan & Contreras, LLC

First Floor: 3,445 sq. ft.

Second Floor: 854 sq. ft.

Total: 4,299 sq. ft.

Width: 95' - 0"

Depth: 67' - 0"

Foundation: Unfinished Basement

Price Code: L1

1-800-850-1491
eplans.com

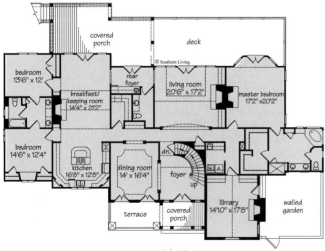

First Floor

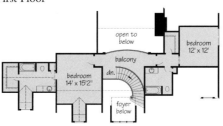

Second Floor

4,302 square feet

Everett Place

PLAN #HPK3700146

Designed by Mitchell Ginn

First Floor: 2,609 sq. ft.

Second Floor: 1,693 sq. ft.

Total: 4,302 sq. ft.

Width: 82' - 0"

Depth: 59' - 0"

Foundation: Unfinished Basement

Price Code: L1

1–800–850–1491
eplans.com

4 *Bedrooms* | 3 *Full Baths* | 1 *Half Bath*

First Floor

Second Floor

Beacon Hill

| 3 *Bedrooms* | 5 *Full Baths* | 1 *Half Bath* |

PLAN #HPK3700147

Designed by Bryan & Contreras, LLC

First Floor: 3,418 sq. ft.

Second Floor: 927 sq. ft.

Total: 4,345 sq. ft.

Width: 116' - 0"

Depth: 65' - 0"

Foundation: Unfinished Basement

Price Code: L2

1–800–850–1491
eplans.com

First Floor

Second Floor

Glendale

PLAN #HPK3700166

Designed by Bryan and Contreras, LLC

First Floor: 3,270 sq. ft.

Second Floor: 1,267 sq. ft.

Total: 4,537 sq. ft.

Width: 91' - 0"

Depth: 71' - 0"

Foundation: Unfinished Basement

Price Code: L1

1–800–850–1491
eplans.com

4 *Bedrooms* | 4 *Full Baths* | 2 *Half Baths*

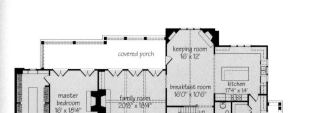

First Floor

Second Floor

Harrod's Creek

4 Bedrooms | **4 Full Baths**

PLAN #HPK3700148

Designed by Cornerstone Group Architects

First Floor: 3,781 sq. ft.

Second Floor: 770 sq. ft.

Total: 4,551 sq. ft.

Width: 126' - 0"

Depth: 86' - 0"

Foundation: Slab

Price Code: L4

1–800–850–1491
eplans.com

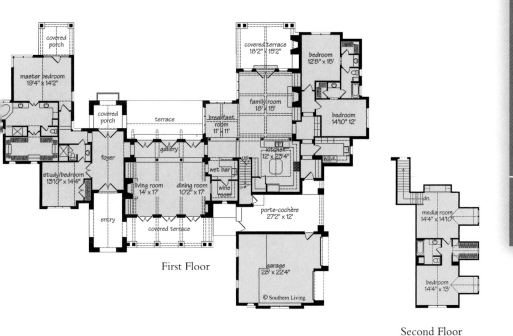

First Floor

Second Floor

Beecham Manor

PLAN #HPK3700149

Designed by Bryan &
Contreras, LLC

First Floor: 3,264 sq. ft.

Second Floor: 1,313 sq. ft.

Total: 4,577 sq. ft.

Width: 114' - 0"

Depth: 63' - 0"

Foundation: Unfinished Basement

Price Code: L2

1–800–850–1491
eplans.com

4 *Bedrooms* | 4 *Full Baths* | 2 *Half Baths*

First Floor

Second Floor

Alouette

| 5 *Bedrooms* | 5 *Full Baths* | 1 *Half Bath* |

PLAN #HPK3700150

Designed by Bryan & Contreras, LLC

First Floor: 3,051 sq. ft.

Second Floor: 1,588 sq. ft.

Total: 4,639 sq. ft.

Width: 102' - 0"

Depth: 87' - 0"

Foundation: Slab

Price Code: L1

1–800–850–1491
eplans.com

First Floor

Second Floor

Rocksprings

PLAN #HPK3700153

Designed by Cornerstone Group Architects

First Floor: 3,845 sq. ft.

Second Floor: 1,088 sq. ft.

Total: 4,933 sq. ft.

Width: 113' – 0"

Depth: 91' – 0"

Foundation: Slab

Price Code: L1

1–800–850–1491
eplans.com

4 *Bedrooms* | 4 *Full Baths* | 1 *Half Bath*

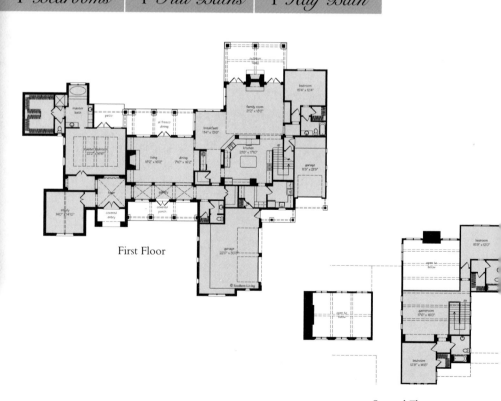

First Floor

Second Floor

Canton Creek

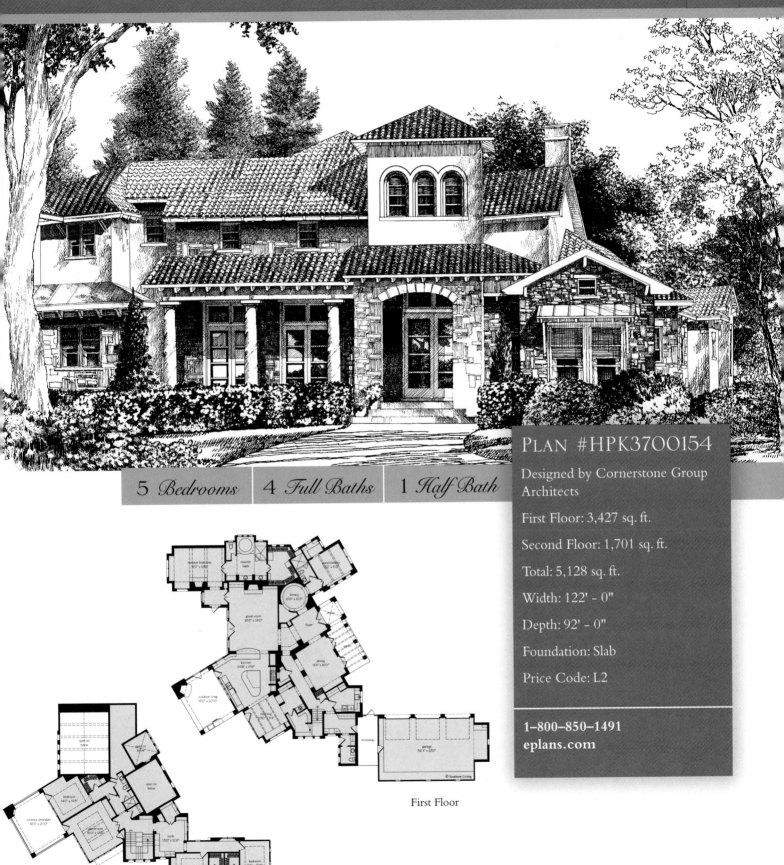

5 *Bedrooms* | **4** *Full Baths* | **1** *Half Bath*

PLAN #HPK3700154

Designed by Cornerstone Group Architects

First Floor: 3,427 sq. ft.

Second Floor: 1,701 sq. ft.

Total: 5,128 sq. ft.

Width: 122' - 0"

Depth: 92' - 0"

Foundation: Slab

Price Code: L2

1–800–850–1491
eplans.com

First Floor

Second Floor

Carriage Park

PLAN #HPK3700155

Designed by Bryan & Contreras, LLC

First Floor: 3,150 sq. ft.

Second Floor: 2,177 sq. ft.

Total: 5,327 sq. ft.

Width: 54' – 0"

Depth: 95' – 0"

Foundation: Slab

Price Code: L4

1–800–850–1491

eplans.com

| 5 *Bedrooms* | 4 *Full Baths* | 1 *Half Bath* |

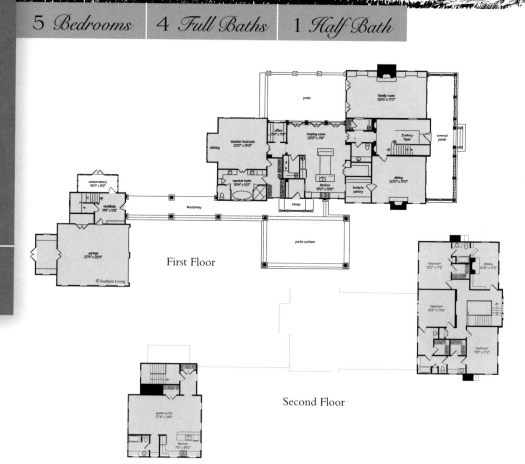

First Floor

Second Floor

Summer Lake

| 4 *Bedrooms* | 4 *Full Baths* | 1 *Half Bath* |

PLAN #HPK3700156

Designed by Bryan & Contreras, LLC

First Floor: 2,850 sq. ft.

Second Floor: 2,528 sq. ft.

Total: 5,378 sq. ft.

Width: 101' - 0"

Depth: 62' - 0"

Foundation: Crawlspace, Slab

Price Code: L4

1-800-850-1491
eplans.com

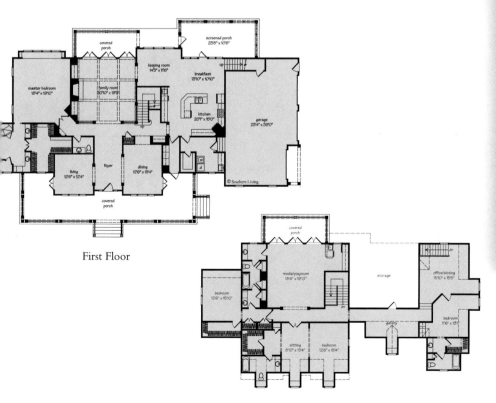

First Floor

Second Floor

Lavendale

PLAN #HPK3700157

Designed by Gary/Ragsdale, Inc.

First Floor: 3,173 sq. ft.

Second Floor: 2,224 sq. ft.

Total: 5,397 sq. ft.

Width: 100' – 0"

Depth: 62' – 0"

Foundation: Slab

Price Code: L2

1–800–850–1491
eplans.com

| 4 *Bedrooms* | 3 *Full Baths* | 1 *Half Bath* |

First Floor

Second Floor

Bella Maison

| 4 *Bedrooms* | 4 *Full Baths* | 1 *Half Bath* |

PLAN #HPK3700158

Designed by Mitchell Ginn

First Floor: 3,412 sq. ft.

Second Floor: 2,048 sq. ft.

Total: 5,460 sq. ft.

Width: 61' - 0"

Depth: 85' - 0"

Foundation: Unfinished Basement

Price Code: L2

1–800–850–1491
eplans.com

First Floor

Second Floor

Avalon

PLAN #HPK3700159

Designed by Spitzmiller and Norris, Inc.

First Floor: 3,317 sq. ft.

Second Floor: 2,150 sq. ft.

Total: 5,467 sq. ft.

Width: 78' - 0"

Depth: 95' - 8"

Foundation: Unfinished Basement

Price Code: L4

1–800–850–1491
eplans.com

| 4 *Bedrooms* | 4 *Full Baths* | 2 *Half Baths* |

Optional Basement

First Floor

Second Floor

Charles Towne Place

| 4 *Bedrooms* | 4 *Full Baths* | 1 *Half Bath* |

PLAN #HPK3700167

Designed by Design Discoveries II

First Floor: 2,463 sq. ft.

Second Floor: 1,564 sq. ft.

Total: 5,501 sq. ft.

Width: 60' – 0"

Depth: 67' – 0"

Foundation: Unfinished Basement

Price Code: L2

1–800–850–1491
eplans.com

Basement

First Floor

Second Floor

Southern Living
SELECTION, CONVENIENCE, SERVICE!

For 20 years, *Southern Living®* magazine has been collecting exclusive home plans from the South's top architects and designers. From formal and elegant traditional homes, to casual and stylish vacation cottages, the *Southern Living* plan collection has been the favorite of the magazine's readers as well as other admirers of southern architecture.

The plans gathered here represent the very best of the Southern Living portfolio. Each home finds a unique balance of historically influenced exteriors—Neoclassical, Colonial, Craftsman, European—and modern approaches to interior layout. Along with beautifully presented formal spaces, each design caters to the comfort and convenience of homeowners with the inclusion of flexible utility spaces, such as mudrooms and offices. Outdoor living areas, present as extended entertaining spaces or as private retreats, are equally important features in the *Southern Living* home.

WHAT YOU'LL GET WITH YOUR ORDER

The contents of each designer's blueprint package is unique, but all contain detailed, high-quality working drawings. You can expect to find the following standard elements in most sets of plans:

ABOUT OUR PLANS

Southern Living working drawings offer a complete conceptual design of our homes. However, our working drawings do not include fully engineered construction documents.

Square Footage Estimates

The heated square footage estimate provided on the small-scale plan does not include the garage, porches, decks, bonus spaces, storage areas, or the basement level. We recommend that your builder verify all of the plan's dimensions and square footage calculations, taking into consideration any modifications or additions.

Also keep in mind that there are several different formulas for calculating square footage, and your builder's estimate may differ slightly from ours.

Estimating Construction Costs

Accurate construction-cost estimates should be made from the working drawings. We suggest consulting with a local builder to provide an estimate of those specific costs. Sometimes your builder can give you a ballpark estimate based on the information provided in the descriptions in this magazine. However, you will need working drawings for more accuracy.

After you order the plans, you may want to get at least two separate estimates from contractors for comparison because many variables can affect cost. The contractor should provide the material quantity lists; costs may vary depending on choice of materials, availability of materials within an area, labor costs, choice of finishes, and degree of detail.

Copy Restrictions and Copyright Information

All *Southern Living* House Plans are protected under the United States Copyright Law. Blueprints may not be resold, copied, or reproduced by any means. When you purchase a blueprint from *Southern Living* House Plans, you are licensed the right to build one residence. *Southern Living* designers and architects retain all rights, title, and ownership to the original design and documents.

What's Included in a Blueprint Package

* **Foundations and floor-framing plans.** This shows the complete foundation layout, including drawings for a basement, slab, or crawlspace. Only one type is included with each plan. Support walls and all necessary dimensions are part of this sheet. Please note that there is no beam layout included with foundation plans.

* **Dimensioned floor plans.** Each floor of the house is shown in detail. The position and dimensions of floors, windows, staircases, and columns are clearly indicated.

* **Suggested electrical plans.** Included are suggestions for the placement of switches, outlets, and fixtures. Local code will dictate exact placement. This will be determined by your builder. Select plans may not include electrical plans.

* **Typical wall section.** This cross section shows a typical wall from footings to roofline.

* **Exterior elevations.** These pages provide drawings of the front, rear, left, and right sides of the house. They also suggest materials for the structure and detail work.

* **Interior elevations.** This includes detailed drawings of cabinets, fireplaces, columns, other built-in units, or suggested trim profiles.

* Suggested exterior and interior finish schedules.
* **Doors and window sizes.**

What's Not Included

* **Heating and plumbing plans.** These plans should be supplied by local subcontractors.

* **Material quantity lists.** Obtain these lists from the contractor you choose or from a local building materials supplier.

* **Architectural and engineering seals.** Some cities and slates require a licensed architect or engineer to review and seal, or officially approve, a blueprint prior to construction due to concerns over energy costs, safety, and other factors. Due to varying local requirements *Southern Living* House Plans is unable to offer these seals. Contract a local building official to find out if such a review is required.

Changing Your Plans

We encourage you to personalize your *Southern Living* House Plan. In an effort to make this process quicker and easier, we offer reproducible prints and electronic CAD files on selected plans. Please note that CAD and Reproducible files come with a one-time construction license and are not returnable.

Rear Elevations

If you would like to see a rear elevation, call toll-free 1–800–850–1491, or visit eplans.com. We offer a complimentary reduced sheet taken directly from our blueprints. This sheet cannot be used for construction purposes, but it will provide a detailed look at the back of the home.

Reverse Plans

Sometimes, to better site a house, it is necessary for the builder to use a reverse set of plans (often called a mirror image or flopped set). If your builder needs a reverse set, order one reverse and the rest standard sets of plans.

Building Codes

Our plans are designed to meet national building standards, but because of varying interpretations, and the fact that codes are subject to change, we cannot warrant compliance with any of the specific building codes and ordinances.

Your local builder or an engineer should review the plan you choose and ensure that it complies with all applicable building codes and subdivision restrictions. We are not responsible for any revisions or interpretations made by third parties involved in the construction of your homes.

BEFORE YOU CALL

You are making a terrific decision to use a pre-drawn house plan—it is one you can make with confidence, knowing that your blueprints are crafted by residential designers and architects, and trusted by builders.

Once you've selected the plan you want—or even if you have questions along the way—our experienced customer service representatives are available to help you navigate the home-building process. To help them provide you with even better service, please consider the following questions before you call:

■ **Have you chosen or purchased your lot?**
If so, please review the building setback requirements of your local building authority before you call. You don't need to have a lot before ordering plans, but if you own land already, please have the width and depth dimensions handy when you call.

■ **Have you chosen a builder?**
Involving your builder in the plan selection and evaluation process may be beneficial. Luckily, builders know they can have confidence with pre-drawn plans because they've been designed for livability, functionality, and typically are builder-proven at successful home sites across the country.

■ **Do you need a construction loan?**
Construction loans are unique because they involve determining the value of something that is not yet constructed. Several lenders offer convenient contstruction-to-permanent loans. It is important to choose a good lending partner—one who will help guide you through the application and appraisal process. Most will even help you evaluate your contractor to ensure reliability and credit worthiness.

■ **How many sets of plans do you need?**
Building a home can typically require a number of sets of blueprints—one for yourself, two or three for the builder and subcontractors, two for the local building department, and one or more for your lender. For this reason, we offer 8-, and Reproducible plan packages, but your best value is the CAD Package, which includes a copy of the digital file used to create the home design. By using CAD software, it is easy to print hard copies of blueprints. Reproducible plans are tremendously flexible in that they allow you to make up to 12 duplicates of the plan so you have enough copies of the plan for everyone involved in the financing and construction of your home.

■ **Do you have to make any changes to meet local building codes?**

While all of our plans are drawn to meet national building codes at the time they were created, many areas required that plans be stamped by a local engineer to certify that they meet local building codes. Building codes are updated frequently and can vary by state, county, city, or municipality. Contact your local building inspection department, office of planning and zoning, or department of permits to determine how your local codes will affect your construction project. The best way to assure that you can make changes to your plan, if necessary, is to purchase a Reproducible or CAD Plan Package.

■ **Has everyone—from family members to contractors—been involved in selecting the plan?**
Building a new home is an exciting process, and using pre-drawn plans is a great way to realize your dreams. Make sure that everyone involved has had an opportunity to review the plan you've selected. While Hanley Wood does have an exchange policy, it's best to be sure all parties agree on your selection before you buy.

CALL TOLL-FREE 1–800–850–1491

Source Key
HPK37

TERMS & CONDITIONS
OUR 90-DAY EXCHANGE POLICY

BUY WITH CONFIDENCE!

As *Southern Living*'s plan fulfillment service, ePlans.com is committed to ensuring your satisfaction with your blueprint order, which is why we offer a 90-day exchange policy. With the exception of Reproducible and CAD Plan Package orders, we will exchange your entire first order for an equal or greater number of blueprints from our plan collection within 90 days of the original order. The entire content of your original order must be returned before an exchange will be processed. Please call our customer service department at 1-888-690-1116 for your return authorization number and shipping instructions. If the returned blueprints look used, redlined, or copied, we will not honor your exchange. Fees for exchanging your blueprints are as follows: 20% of the amount of the original order, plus the difference in cost if exchanging for a design in a higher price bracket or less the difference in cost if exchanging for a design in a lower price bracket. (Because they can be copied, Reproducible or CAD blueprints are not exchangeable or refundable.) Please call for current postage and handling prices. Shipping and handling charges are not refundable.

ARCHITECTURAL AND ENGINEERING SEALS
Some cities and states now require that a licensed architect or engineer review and "seal" a blueprint, or officially approve it, prior to construction. Prior to application for a building permit or the start of actual construction, we strongly advise that you consult your local building official who can tell you if such a review is required.

LOCAL BUILDING CODES AND ZONING REQUIREMENTS
Each plan was designed to meet or exceed the requirements of a nationally recognized model building code in effect at the time and place the plan was drawn. Typically plans designed after the year 2000 conform to the International Residential Building Code (IRC 2000 or 2003). The IRC is comprised of portions of the three major codes below. Plans drawn before 2000 conform to one of the three recognized building codes in effect at the time: Building Officials and Code Administrators (BOCA)

CALL TOLL FREE 1-800-850-1491 OR VISIT EPLANS.COM

International, Inc.; the Southern Building Code Congress International, (SBCCI) Inc.; the International Conference of Building Officials (ICBO); or the Council of American Building Officials (CABO).

Because of the great differences in geography and climate throughout the United States and Canada, each state, county, and municipality has its own building codes, zone requirements, ordinances, and building regulations. Your plan may need to be modified to comply with local requirements. In addition, you may need to obtain permits or inspections from local governments before and in the course of construction. We authorize the use of the blueprints on the express condition that you consult a local licensed architect or engineer of your choice prior to beginning construction and strictly comply with all local building codes, zoning requirements, and other applicable laws, regulations, ordinances, and requirements. Notice: Plans for homes to be built in Nevada must be redrawn by a Nevada-registered professional. Consult your local building official for more information on this subject.

TERMS AND CONDITIONS
These designs are protected under the terms of United States Copyright Law and may not be copied or reproduced in any way, by any means, unless you have purchased a Reproducible Plan Package and signed the accompanying license to modify and copy the plan, which clearly indicates your right to modify, copy, or reproduce. We authorize the use of your chosen design as an aid in the construction of ONE (1) single-family home only. You may not use this design to build a second dwelling or multiple dwellings without purchasing another blueprint or blueprints or paying additional design fees.

DISCLAIMER
The designers we work with have put substantial care and effort into the creation of their blueprints. However, because we cannot provide on-site consultation, supervision, and control over actual construction, and because of the great variance in local building requirements, building practices, and soil, seismic, weather, and other conditions, WE MAKE NO WARRANTY OF ANY KIND, EXPRESS OR IMPLIED, WITH RESPECT TO THE CONTENT OR USE OF THE BLUEPRINTS, INCLUDING BUT NOT LIMITED TO ANY WARRANTY OF MERCHANTABILITY OR OF FITNESS FOR A PARTICULAR PURPOSE. ITEMS, PRICES, TERMS, AND CONDITIONS ARE SUBJECT TO CHANGE WITHOUT NOTICE.

IMPORTANT COPYRIGHT NOTICE
From the Council of Publishing Home Designers

Blueprints for residential construction (or working drawings, as they are often called in the industry) are copyrighted intellectual property, protected under the terms of the United States Copyright Law and, therefore, cannot be copied legally for use in building. The following are some guidelines to help you get what you need to build your home, without violating copyright law:

1. HOME PLANS ARE COPYRIGHTED
Just like books, movies, and songs, home plans receive protection under the federal copyright laws. The copyright laws prevent anyone, other than the copyright owner, from reproducing, modifying, or reusing the plans or design without permission of the copyright owner.

2. DO NOT COPY DESIGNS OR FLOOR PLANS FROM ANY PUBLICATION, ELECTRONIC MEDIA, OR EXISTING HOME
It is illegal to copy, change, or redraw home designs found in a plan book, CDROM or on the Internet. The right to modify plans is one of the exclusive rights of copyright. It is also illegal to copy or redraw a constructed home that is protected by copyright, even if you have never seen the plans for the home. If you find a plan or home that you like, you must purchase a set of plans from an authorized source. The plans may not be lent, given away, or sold by the purchaser.

3. DO NOT USE PLANS TO BUILD MORE THAN ONE HOUSE
The original purchaser of house plans is typically licensed to build a single home from the plans. Building more than one home from the plans without permission is an infringement of the home designer's copyright. The purchase of a multiple-set package of plans is for the construction of a single home only. The purchase of additional sets of plans does not grant the right to construct more than one home.

4. HOUSE PLANS IN THE FORM OF BLUEPRINTS OR BLACKLINES CANNOT BE COPIED OR REPRODUCED
Plans, blueprints, or blacklines, unless they are reproducibles, cannot be copied or reproduced without prior written consent of the copyright owner. Copy shops and blueprinters are prohibited from making copies of these plans without the copyright release letter you receive with reproducible plans.

5. HOUSE PLANS IN THE FORM OF BLUEPRINTS OR BLACKLINES CANNOT BE REDRAWN
Plans cannot be modified or redrawn without first obtaining the copyright owner's permission. With your purchase of plans, you are licensed to make non-structural changes by "red-lining" the purchased plans. If you need to make structural changes or need to redraw the plans for any reason, you must purchase a reproducible set of plans (see topic 6) which includes a license to modify the plans. Blueprints do not come with a license to make structural changes or to redraw the plans. You may not reuse or sell the modified design.

6. REPRODUCIBILE HOME PLANS
Reproducible plans (for example sepias, mylars, CAD files, electronic files, and vellums) come with a license to make modifications to the plans. Once modified, the plans can be taken to a local copy shop or blueprinter to make up to 10 or 12 copies of the plans to use in the construction of a single home. Only one home can be constructed from any single purchased set of reproducible plans either in original form or as modified. The license to modify and copy must be completed and returned before the plan will be shipped.

7. MODIFIED DESIGNS CANNOT BE REUSED
Even if you are licensed to make modifications to a copyrighted design, the modified design is not free from the original designer's copyright. The sale or reuse of the modified design is prohibited. Also, be aware that any modification to plans relieves the original designer from liability for design defects and voids all warranties expressed or implied.

8. WHO IS RESPONSIBLE FOR COPYRIGHT INFRINGEMENT?
Any party who participates in a copyright violation may be responsible including the purchaser, designers, architects, engineers, drafters, homeowners, builders, contractors, sub-contractors, copy shops, blueprinters, developers, and real estate agencies. It does not matter whether or not the individual knows that a violation is being committed. Ignorance of the law is not a valid defense.

9. PLEASE RESPECT HOME DESIGN COPYRIGHTS
In the event of any suspected violation of a copyright, or if there is any uncertainty about the plans purchased, the publisher, architect, designer, or the Council of Publishing Home Designers (www.cphd.org) should be contacted before proceeding. Awards are some-times offered for information about home design copyright infringement.

10. PENALTIES FOR INFRINGEMENT
Penalties for violating a copyright may be severe. The responsible parties are required to pay actual damages caused by the infringement (which may be substantial), plus any profits made by the infringer commissions to include all profits from the sale of any home built from an infringing design. The copyright law also allows for the recovery of statutory damages, which may be as high as $150,000 for each infringement. Finally, the infringer may be required to pay legal fees which often exceed the damages.

PAGE	PLAN #	PLAN NAME	PRICE CODE	8-SET PACKAGE	REPRODUCIBLE PACKAGE	CAD PACKAGE
6	HPK3700001	SAND MOUNTAIN HOUSE	L4	$1,440	$1,850	
11	HPK3700002	BANNING COURT	C1	$810	$1,000	
12	HPK3700003	ASHLEY RIVER COTTAGE	C1	$810	$1,000	
13	HPK3700004	ELLSWORTH COTTAGE	C1	$810	$1,000	
14	HPK3700005	ASHTON	C1	$810	$1,000	
15	HPK3700006	SILVERHILL	C3	$910	$1,145	
16	HPK3700007	BUCKSPORT COTTAGE	C1	$810	$1,000	
17	HPK3700008	GRESHAM CREEK COTTAGE	A3	$690	$870	
18	HPK3700009	ELIZABETH'S PLACE	C1	$810	$1,000	
19	HPK3700010	FORESTDALE	C3	$910	$1,145	$1,915
20	HPK3700011	COTTON HILL COTTAGE	C1	$810	$1,000	
21	HPK3700012	MISS MAGGIE'S HOUSE	C1	$810	$1,000	
22	HPK3700013	WILLIAMS BLUFF	C1	$810	$1,000	
23	HPK3700014	LOWCOUNTRY COTTAGE	C1	$810	$1,000	
24	HPK3700015	MAPLE HILL	C1	$810	$1,000	
25	HPK3700016	AIKEN RIDGE	C3	$910	$1,145	
26	HPK3700017	NEW RUSTIC OAKS	C3	$910	$1,145	
27	HPK3700018	BRADLEY HOUSE	C3	$910	$1,145	
28	HPK3700019	NEW ROUND HILL	C3	$910	$1,145	
29	HPK3700020	AMBERVIEW WAY	C1	$810	$1,000	
30	HPK3700021	ANGEL OAK POINT	C1	$810	$1,000	
31	HPK3700022	RIVER VIEW COTTAGE	C3	$910	$1,145	
32	HPK3700023	FRANKLIN HOUSE	L4	$1,440	$1,850	
33	HPK3700024	WINNSBORO HEIGHTS	C1	$810	$1,000	
34	HPK3700025	VALENSOLE	C3	$910	$1,145	$1,915
35	HPK3700026	MABRY COTTAGE	C3	$910	$1,145	
36	HPK3700027	PEACHTREE COTTAGE	C3	$910	$1,145	
37	HPK3700028	LAKESIDE COTTAGE	A4	$750	$935	
38	HPK3700029	PENNINGTON POINT	C3	$910	$1,145	
39	HPK3700030	NEW OXFORD	L1	$1,115	$1,390	
40	HPK3700033	MONTEREAU	L1	$1,115	$1,390	
41	HPK3700032	THE PARK	C3	$910	$1,145	
42	HPK3700031	BEAUMONT	C3	$910	$1,145	
43	HPK3700034	WHITESTONE	C3	$910	$1,145	
44	HPK3700035	WESTBURY PARK	C3	$910	$1,145	
45	HPK3700036	STONEBRIDGE COTTAGE	C3	$910	$1,145	
46	HPK3700037	MOORE'S CREEK	C3	$910	$1,145	
47	HPK3700038	BELHAVEN PLACE	C3	$910	$1,145	$1,915
48	HPK3700039	PINE HILL COTTAGE	C3	$910	$1,145	
49	HPK3700040	SEA ISLAND HOUSE	SQ5	N/A	$2,190	
54	HPK3700161	BLUFF HAVEN	C1	$810	$1,000	
55	HPK3700071	POPPY POINT	C3	$910	$1,145	$1,915
56	HPK3700042	COTTAGE OF THE YEAR	L4	$1,440	$1,850	
57	HPK3700054	NEW LYNWOOD	C3	$910	$1,145	
58	HPK3700043	NEW MEADOWLARK	C3	$910	$1,145	
59	HPK3700044	POPLAR CREEK COTTAGE	C3	$910	$1,145	
60	HPK3700045	MANDEVILLE PLACE	C3	$910	$1,145	
61	HPK3700046	NEW WYNTUCK	C1	$810	$1,000	
62	HPK3700047	SPRING LAKE COTTAGE	L4	$1,440	$1,850	$3,140
63	HPK3700048	ALTA VISTA	L4	$1,440	$1,850	$3,140
64	HPK3700049	OVERTON PLACE	C3	$910	$1,145	$1,915
65	HPK3700050	TURNBALL PARK	C3	$910	$1,145	
66	HPK3700051	ELDERBERRY PLACE	C3	$910	$1,145	
67	HPK3700052	ARBOR VIEW	C3	$910	$1,145	$1,915
68	HPK3700053	GRISSOM TRAIL	C1	$810	$1,000	$1,735

PAGE	PLAN #	PLAN NAME	PRICE CODE	8-SET PACKAGE	REPRODUCIBLE PACKAGE	CAD PACKAGE
69	HPK3700060	McKenzie Cottage	C1	$810	$1,000	
70	HPK3700057	New Cooper's Bluff	L1	$1,115	$1,390	
71	HPK3700162	Kilburne	C3	$910	$1,145	
72	HPK3700058	New Holly Springs	L1	$1,115	$1,390	
73	HPK3700059	New Shannon	C3	$910	$1,145	
74	HPK3700061	Northridge	C3	$910	$1,145	$1,915
75	HPK3700063	Iberville	L1	$1,115	$1,390	
76	HPK3700064	Fairfield Place	C3	$910	$1,145	
77	HPK3700065	Wesley	C3	$910	$1,145	
78	HPK3700067	River Bend Farmhouse	L4	$1,440	$1,850	$3,140
79	HPK3700068	New Brookhaven	C3	$910	$1,145	
80	HPK3700062	Arden Gate	L2	$1,195	$1,515	
81	HPK3700069	Allendale	L1	$1,115	$1,390	
82	HPK3700066	Louisiana Garden Cottage	C3	$910	$1,145	
83	HPK3700070	Cumberland	C3	$910	$1,145	
84	HPK3700163	Bedford Cottage	L1	$1,115	$1,390	
85	HPK3700072	The Juliette	L1	$1,115	$1,390	
86	HPK3700073	Chestnut Hill	L4	$1,440	$1,850	
87	HPK3700074	Poplar Grove	L4	$1,440	$1,850	
92	HPK3700075	Inanda House	L4	$1,440	$1,850	
93	HPK3700076	Woodlawn	C3	$910	$1,145	
94	HPK3700077	Clayfield Place	L1	$1,115	$1,390	
95	HPK3700078	The Orchard House	L4	$1,440	$1,850	
96	HPK3700079	Brookwood Cottage	L1	$1,115	$1,390	
97	HPK3700083	Presque Isle	C3	$910	$1,145	
98	HPK3700081	Myrtle Grove	C3	$910	$1,145	
99	HPK3700080	Live Oak Cottage	L4	$1,440	$1,850	
100	HPK3700089	Scarborough	C3	$910	$1,145	$1,915
101	HPK3700082	The Jefferson	C3	$910	$1,145	
102	HPK3700084	River Bluff	L2	$1,195	$1,515	
103	HPK3700117	Lamberth Way	C3	$910	$1,145	
104	HPK3700085	2006 Cooking Light Fit House	L2	$1,195	$1,515	
105	HPK3700164	Bankston	C3	$910	$1,145	
106	HPK3700087	The Shoals	C3	$910	$1,145	
107	HPK3700088	Shook Hill	L1	$1,115	$1,390	
108	HPK3700090	Howell Park	L1	$1,115	$1,390	
109	HPK3700091	New Willow Grove	L1	$1,115	$1,390	
110	HPK3700092	Crescent Hill	C3	$910	$1,145	$1,915
111	HPK3700093	Biddleford	C3	$910	$1,145	
112	HPK3700094	Van Buren	C3	$910	$1,145	
113	HPK3700095	Monet House	C3	$910	$1,145	
114	HPK3700097	Denham Springs	L2	$1,195	$1,515	
115	HPK3700098	Clenney Point	L1	$1,115	$1,390	
116	HPK3700099	Lexington	C3	$910	$1,145	$1,915
117	HPK3700100	Aaronwood	L1	$1,115	$1,390	
118	HPK3700101	Brookfield	L4	$1,440	$1,850	$3,140
119	HPK3700102	Stones River	L4	$1,440	$1,850	$3,140
124	HPK3700103	Kinsley Place	SQ3	N/A	$1,931	$3,299
125	HPK3700104	Vernon Hill	L4	$1,440	$1,850	
126	HPK3700106	Danbury Oaks	L1	$1,115	$1,390	
127	HPK3700107	Crestview Park	L1	$1,115	$1,390	
128	HPK3700108	Abberley Lane	L4	$1,440	$1,850	
129	HPK3700109	Rucker Place	L1	$1,115	$1,390	
130	HPK3700110	Newberry Park	L4	$1,440	$1,850	
131	HPK3700111	Avington Place	L1	$1,115	$1,390	

PAGE	PLAN #	PLAN NAME	PRICE CODE	8-SET PACKAGE	REPRODUCIBLE PACKAGE	CAD PACKAGE
132	HPK3700112	CYPRESS GARDEN	L1	$1,115	$1,390	$2,500
133	HPK3700152	LINDEN	L1	$1,115	$1,390	
134	HPK3700113	SMYTHE PARK HOUSE	L4	$1,440	$1,850	
135	HPK3700115	AMELIA PLACE	L4	$1,440	$1,850	
136	HPK3700114	BELFIELD BEND	L2	$1,195	$1,515	
137	HPK3700116	CHATHAM HALL	L2	$1,195	$1,515	
138	HPK3700151	BRENTHAVEN	L4	$1,440	$1,850	
139	HPK3700105	BELVEDERE	L1	$1,115	$1,390	
140	HPK3700118	ASH LAWN	L2	$1,195	$1,515	
141	HPK3700119	ANSLEY PARK	L1	$1,115	$1,390	
142	HPK3700120	SWANNANOA RIVER HOUSE	L4	$1,440	$1,850	$3,140
143	HPK3700121	WESTON HOUSE	L4	$1,440	$1,850	
144	HPK3700131	CRABAPPLE COTTAGE	L4	$1,440	$1,850	
145	HPK3700056	STERETT SPRINGS	L1	$1,115	$1,390	
146	HPK3700122	BRITTINGHAM	L1	$1,115	$1,390	
147	HPK3700123	GREYWELL COTTAGE	L4	$1,440	$1,850	
148	HPK3700124	ROCKWELL HOUSE	L1	$1,115	$1,390	
149	HPK3700125	BRADEN HOUSE	L4	$1,440	$1,850	
150	HPK3700126	SAGEWICK HOUSE	L1	$1,115	$1,390	
151	HPK3700127	CLAREMONT	L1	$1,115	$1,390	$2,500
152	HPK3700128	WHITFIELD II	L1	$1,115	$1,390	
153	HPK3700096	MULBERRY PARK	L4	$1,440	$1,850	
154	HPK3700130	SABINE RIVER COTTAGE	L2	$1,195	$1,515	
155	HPK3700132	COLONIAL LAKE COTTAGE	L1	$1,115	$1,390	
156	HPK3700133	WALKER'S BLUFF	L4	$1,440	$1,850	$3,140
157	HPK3700134	PINE GLEN	L2	$1,195	$1,515	$2,575
158	HPK3700135	SIENNA PARK	L2	$1,195	$1,515	
159	HPK3700136	FOREST GLEN	C4	$970	$1,225	
160	HPK3700129	LUBERON	L1	$1,115	$1,390	$2,500
161	HPK3700165	TRAVIS RIDGE	L4	$1,440	$1,850	
162	HPK3700138	RIDDLEY PARK	L2	$1,195	$1,515	
163	HPK3700139	CARTER HALL	L1	$1,115	$1,390	
164	HPK3700140	HARWOOD PARK	L1	$1,115	$1,390	
165	HPK3700141	WILMINGTON PLACE	L1	$1,115	$1,390	
166	HPK3700142	STANTON COURT	L1	$1,115	$1,390	
167	HPK3700143	CAMBRIDGE	L1	$1,115	$1,390	$2,500
168	HPK3700144	STRATHMORE	L1	$1,115	$1,390	
169	HPK3700145	WHITFIELD	L1	$1,115	$1,390	
170	HPK3700146	EVERETT PLACE	L1	$1,115	$1,390	
171	HPK3700147	BEACON HILL	L2	$1,195	$1,515	
172	HPK3700166	GLENDALE	L1	$1,115	$1,390	
173	HPK3700148	HARROD'S CREEK	L4	$1,440	$1,850	
174	HPK3700149	BEECHAM MANOR	L2	$1,195	$1,515	
175	HPK3700150	ALOUETTE	L1	$1,115	$1,390	
176	HPK3700153	ROCKSPRINGS	L1	$1,115	$1,390	
177	HPK3700154	CANTON CREEK	L2	$1,195	$1,515	
178	HPK3700155	CARRIAGE PARK	L4	$1,440	$1,850	
179	HPK3700156	SUMMER LAKE	L4	$1,440	$1,850	
180	HPK3700157	LAVENDALE	L2	$1,195	$1,515	
181	HPK3700158	BELLA MAISON	L2	$1,195	$1,515	
182	HPK3700159	AVALON	L4	$1,440	$1,850	
183	HPK3700167	CHARLES TOWNE PLACE	L2	$1,195	$1,515	
192	HPK3700160	CENTENNIAL HOUSE	L4	$1,440	$1,850	$3,140

Centennial House

PLAN #HPK3700160

Designed by Spitzmiller and Norris, Inc.

First Floor: 3,875 sq. ft.

Second Floor: 1,701 sq. ft.

Total: 5,576 sq. ft.

Width: 154' - 0"

Depth: 71' - 0"

Foundation: Unfinished Basement

Price Code: L4

1–800–850–1491
eplans.com

| 5 *Bedrooms* | 5 *Full Baths* | 2 *Half Baths* |

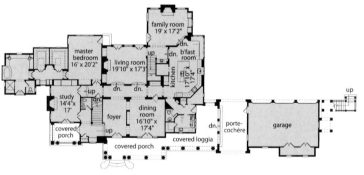

First Floor

Second Floor